The Joy of Running
SLED DOGS
A Step-by-Step Guide

The Joy of Running SLED DOGS

A Step-by-Step Guide

by Noël K. Flanders

1989

Alpine Publications Inc.

THE JOY OF RUNNING SLED DOGS
A Step-by-Step Guide

ISBN Number 0-931866-39-1

Cover photo by: Ollie Wicks
Text photos by author unless otherwise noted.
Cover and book design by Joan Harris.

Printed in the United States of America.

To the many experienced mushers who have worked hard to train their dogs to run, and all the beginning mushers about to learn a wonderful new sport.

Contents

Foreword ix

Acknowledgments xi

The Joy of Running Sled Dogs 1

Characteristics of the Sled Dog 5
Breeds best suited for sledding • Large vs. small dogs • Body structure • Legs and feet

The Strength of the Sled Dog 14
Competitive weight pulling • Discussion

Introduction to Equipment 18
Harnesses and their history • Different types • Fit • How to put on • How to order • Ganglines

Carts and Wheeled Rigs 30
The Lightweight Cart • Steering • Brakes

Sleds 34
Sprint Sleds • Toboggan Sled • Freight Sled • Parts of a Sled

Snow Hooks and Quick-Release **43**
Attaching the Snow Hook • The Quick Release

Transporting and Restraining Your Team **49**
How to make a chain stake-out • Dog boxes

Clothing **57**
The wind chill factor • Jackets • Gloves • Face mask • Underwear
• Boots • Hats

The Team **63**
The making of a team • Lead dogs • Point or swing dogs • Team
dogs • Wheelers

Training **69**
Basic Training • The first ride • Tangles

Lead Dog Training **78**
Making the trail • Putting the lead dog through his paces

Riding the Sled **83**
Helping the team • Cornering • Stopping

Racing **87**
The Start • Trail markers • Etiquette • Sprint Racing • Middle
distance races • Long distance races • Family sport

Caring for the Sled Dog **97**
Foot care • Ice and snow problems • Booties • Outdoor shelters

Appendix **103**
Newsletters and magazines • Directory of outfitters

Glossary **105**

Foreword

Once I got out of the starting chute and took my turn gliding over the trail, I could really appreciate the glory of it all—flying down a hill at full speed, approaching another team head on as the dogs play their own version of chicken. Neither driver wants to give up any speed or time but no one can really say if the dogs will pass each other or simply pile head on into a massive tangle of fur, feet, sleds and rope. At the last second the dogs veer off in different directions and the mushers fly past with inches to spare, looking forward to another exciting encounter up the trail.

Start with 40 to 50 vehicles ranging from the polished and plush of the rich and serious racer to the not so pretty "beaters" like my rusty ten year old Chevy. Park this automotive menagerie along a snow packed road and then watch as humans of all sizes, shapes and ages emerge wearing their particular choice of winter clothing. They all have their own idea of how a "musher" should look from expensive boots to tennis shoes, wool pants to blue jeans, or hats made of dog hair. The fashion statement of this group is . . . well, unique. At this point we already have enough entertainment on hand to rival any good state fair with sideshows, and we haven't even unloaded the dogs. And dogs, and dogs, and dogs! I figure there were over 250 canines with this mobile dog pound and they are all barking and howling in anticipation of the big race.

Throughout all of this, the woman who promised to love honor and balance my checkbook has been staying close to the truck wondering just how much of our dream house has been sacrificed for my involvement in this insanity.

I especially enjoyed the opportunity to help out a fellow musher in need. It was a gratifying experience to know I could help when I saw a team and sled with no driver coming my way. I stopped my team and gallantly stepped off to grab the runaways knowing how pleased their driver would be to find his/her sled with the snow hook firmly set. Only one small problem. In my desire to serve mankind, I forgot to set my own snow hook and before I could say "good Samaritan" my team was headed south—fast. As I tried to run up a snowy hill to catch a team that has suddenly changed from average to lightening fast (I've always been a hopeless optimist), I tried to think how I would explain to the coach that I lost my team. She'll probably disown me in embarrassment unless I can convince her it was a critical emergency. (Let's see, the driver was tangled in the ropes and being drug, I had to save him! No, she'll never buy that one.)

Fortunately some equally brave but more experienced musher snagged my team and set the hook for me, allowing me to catch the team just before I suffered cardiac arrest. I managed to finish the race with a respectable showing and proudly set about mingling with other mushers! I wondered what type of fur animal hat I had now earned the right to wear. Maybe I could dress in a full bear skin . . .

Well, it's over! My first real sled dog race has come and gone, my bruises and aching muscles are healing and the dogs are resting. As I look back at this event, the word "experience" seems appropriate. The dictionary (American Heritage, second college edition) says experience is "an understanding of the mind, senses and emotions through which knowledge or skill is gained. An event lived through!" Sounds like a sled race to me!

Randy Cumley
1988

Acknowledgments

A special thanks to Peggy and Ed Samberson for putting up with me during all the training mishaps we have had while running our sled dogs in the wee hours of the morning. Also, thank you to Frank and Nettie Hall for all their words of wisdom and help.

I would also like to extend a very special thank you to Ollie Wicks of *First Photo* in Colorado Springs for assistance with the photography. Without you, Ollie, this book would be only a dream. Thanks!

1
The Joy
of Running Sled Dogs

Imagine a cold winter morning, the sun is brightly shining on fresh-fallen snow, and you have been faithfully training your team of sled dogs since early fall. And now it is time to prove yourselves a worthy challenge to other teams on the racing circuit.

Today is the big day—the first sled dog race of the season!

You and your loyal companions have spent many long hours together on the trail, training late into the night, or very early in the morning before going to work. There were times you trained during a blizzard you wished would end, but didn't. Fingertips have been frostbitten, because there were times when a dog had to be changed to a different position on the team and you had to take your gloves off to feel the snaps.

Hundreds of dogs are barking all around, and some of the spectators have dropped by and complimented you on your pretty sled dogs. Smiling, you reply, "Thanks," and then continue getting ready for the big moment.

You ask some of the other drivers to help get your team to the starting area. You wait. There are two teams in front of you and you make a last minute check of dogs and equipment. The excitement grows, your heart is pounding. Every muscle in your body quivers. You are scared to death because it's all so new: the trail, the procedure, all the unknowns lurking before you on the untried run. Yes, every trail was new the first time you ran it, but even this knowledge isn't particularly calming. Then suddenly there's no more time for thinking . . . now *you* are at the starting line. As officials make sure the brushbow is at the orange marker, you pet each of the dogs, telling them it is going to be a fun run. Ruffing up the leader's fur, you turn and take your position at the sled. Checking your snow hook, the dog-bag, the extra tug line—yes, everything is ready. *You're* ready. The countdown begins . . .

"FIVE . . . FOUR . . . THREE . . . TWO . . . ONE . . . GO!"

"HIKE," you call out to the dogs. "Let's go," and you're off and running.

As you slip along a glistening trail all the fear is gone. The serenity of being alone with the team in the quiet winter wonderland makes all the hard work worthwhile. You glide along the freshly groomed trail that winds through the trees along the lake. You climb a steep hill, and fly down the other side. Yes, that was a real challenge, but you made it. Grinning to yourself you know that this is what you've waited for all these months and for which you trained so hard.

Finishing the race with a smile, you're proud of your team and yourself. You finished your first race, still had the team, didn't lose them on any of the sharp turns, and turned in a pretty good time for the run. You have done well. But suddenly it isn't winning that's important, it's the way the race was run and the special relationship between you and your dogs. That's what matters.

The joy of running a team of sled dogs down a snow-packed trail early in the morning is the most fantastic way I know to start out a day and now *you* can have such a day. Plan a winter camping trip and load up the dogs, pack everything in your sled and head for the high country. Include a little ice fishing, or perhaps just relax with your family. If you're not into ice fishing you may want to explore new trails. Getting away from all the hustle and bustle of everyday chores is great for mind and body.

It's a lot of fun getting together with a few other drivers and their families to go on an overnight camping trip with your teams. During the day you can take different trails and explore areas you might otherwise never see. For instance, Yellowstone Park is a great place to visit in the winter; there are snowmobile and cross-country trails throughout the park. There is also a snow-cat that will bring in equipment and passengers to the main lodge. You'll need special permission to bring the dogs, but winter tourists are always welcome, whether human or canine. Contact the rangers' station at Old Faithful to make reservations.

Once you become proficient in dog-sledding and have some basic winter survival training, you can go almost anywhere there are snowpacked trails to follow. There are 150 miles of groomed snowmobile trails at Red Feather Lakes in northern Colorado—perfect for running sled dogs. You can enjoy winter camping and ice fishing as well as snowmobiling. This is an excellent place to train a team or just go for the fun of it.

An exhuberant start!

A tired five-dog team of Siberian Huskies. The driver (me) was a happy-camper as she finished her first sled dog race.

3

If you like to cross-country ski, think how much fun it would be to have a dog pull you effortlessly along with a tow rope. Your dog can also carry lunch in a saddlebag.

Winter is not the only time to enjoy your sled dogs. In summer you can have a lot of fun running them with a three-wheeled cart. And there are many other things to do with these dogs after you have trained them. For instance, how about back-packing with them? Saddlebags for dogs are available in three sizes: small, medium, and large. In these bags the dog can carry one-third of his weight. He can carry his own dog food, other small items, and provide a lot of company on a hike through the wilderness.

There are beautiful trails to follow in the summer such as the one that has been built over the Continental Divide from south of Denver to Durango, Colorado. This trail is over 480 miles long and has taken a volunteer group over 14 years to construct. It meanders among 10,000-foot mountain passes, old mining towns, historical sites, and fire-blackened forests. Areas like this are wonderful for family vacations since the trail is constructed so that anyone can hike it, and there are huts along the way to provide shelter. In addition the route passes near towns and cities so hikers can easily replenish supplies. More details can be obtained from the Denver Chamber of Commerce.

With a little *imagination*, one could find many ways to enjoy "man's best friend." Running dogs is a lot of fun, summer or winter, so go for it!

2
Characteristics
of the Sled Dog

The sled dog should weigh between thirty-five and sixty pounds, have a desire to run and a lot of energy. If they have a natural desire to run, most dogs can be trained to pull a sled or a skier.

Keep in mind the size of your dog in comparison to the load he will be pulling. If he's small, he may need a little help; if he's larger, you may get to ride the sled more often.

BREEDS BEST SUITED FOR SLEDDING

The most common dogs running on today's circuit are the Siberian Husky, Alaskan Husky and the Lab/hound mix. I have seen teams of Irish Setters that ran beautifully, and I've also seen Dalmatians and a Standard Poodle run. The Poodle was much too smart for pulling a sled, so he just ran in between the lines and let the others do the work. There is a team of Coonhounds in the Northeast that does very well, but you can hear them coming for miles.

In general, the dogs that are winning are hounds mixed with Siberian Huskies, Targhee hounds, or Saluki hounds mixed with a Nordic-type dog. Even a Labrador-Siberian mix is not uncommon and is quite fast. The Alaskan Husky is a village dog often with the markings of the Siberian. This dog was developed in Alaska by Indians and Eskimos, who took their fastest dogs and bred them to other fast dogs to produce a racing animal.

The Alaskan Huskies are usually faster than the Siberians and are proving themselves on the race circuits of Colorado, the Northwest, and Northwest Alaska. A new program called SEPP (Siberian Evaluation Performance Project) headed by Dick Moulton, has been established to evaluate Siberians and an evaluator judges each dog on the team for his stamina, speed and performance. Each dog that completes this testing is given a certificate depending on his performance. This new clinic is intended to upgrade the Siberian Husky to the quality it was when Seppala was running them. If you have a pure-bred Siberian Husky and would like to know more about the SEPP program, contact the International Sled Dog Association.

THE LARGER DOG VERSUS THE SMALLER DOG

One might think that because a dog is large, he could pull heavier loads and run faster, but that is not necessarily so!

The larger-boned dog (Alaskan Malamute, German Shepherd, Labrador Retriever) weighing over sixty pounds, compares to a draft horse running against a thoroughbred in the Kentucky Derby. The heavy dogs can run long distances but at a much slower pace than the smaller breeds. Alaskan Malamutes are noted for their endurance, can go forever at three or four miles an hour, and are called "freighting dogs." These dogs are used for distance running and carrying heavy loads. They are also used in competitive weight-pulling contests for they have incredible strength. Some die-hard racers will run the Malamutes in today's racing circuits; they aren't very fast, but they make an impressive looking team.

The smaller dog weighing between thirty and sixty pounds (Siberian Husky, Alaskan Husky, Eskimo dog, Dalmatian, Targhee Hound, Irish Setter, Norwegian Elkhound, and the Samoyed), will usually have an easier time pulling a sled. He is more agile and has more flexibility in his legs. A dog with a springy trot does not tire as easily as a dog with a flat trot. This springy action shows good muscle control and agility.

Don't underestimate the strength of the smaller dog. If you were to race two teams of five dogs, one team comprised of dogs weighing forty-five to fifty pounds and the second team consisting of dogs weighing eighty pounds or more, the smaller team would probably win. This is true even if they carry the same amount of weight on the sled and go the same distance.

BODY STRUCTURE

The body structure of the sled dog is of great importance. Most mushers agree that long-legged, streamlined dogs such as the Hound/Alaskan,

An Alaskan Husky. Note the sloping back and the angulation of the hind legs. When the front leg is brought up, there is almost a straight line from the elbow to the chest bone. This will give the dog a good reach as the leg comes forward. The coat is very short, yet has a thick undercoat. Notice the Siberian facial markings. This is also a good example of how the harness should fit. When the gangline is attached to the small loop at the back near the tail, this harness will fit perfectly.

The Afghan Hound is another dog that can be run. He is very intelligent. His hair must be trimmed close so as not to collect snowballs in the soft hair. He is quite fast for short distances.

The Airdale can be run, but his feet will need extra care because untrimmed hair will collect snowballs and the soft tissue between his toes is easily bruised. Airdales are friendly, love to please their owner, and are fairly good at pulling a sled.

Hound/Lab, Hound/Siberian or the Alaskan Husky are best suited for the fast, short races. Any of these long-legged dogs dogs will accelerate to a fast pace for a few miles, since they have tremendous thrust from their long, slender legs. However, these dogs, with the exception of the Alaskan Husky, cannot go for long distances because they usually do not have the endurance. They are built for speed, and the sprint races are short enough to allow them to do exceptionally well. When a driver mixes a hound-type dog with a Nordic breed, he is breeding for speed and the ability to withstand colder temperatures. The Nordic dog has a heavier coat and good feet, and this, coupled with the added speed of the hound, produces a winner. The dogs that are running on today's circuit are very fast and getting faster each year.

I was talking to some of the veteran drivers recently about how we keep improving our dogs and getting faster teams but are maintaining the same position we held last year. Everyone else is doing the same thing! As a Siberian Husky fan, I will never be in the top money with the hounds in the short sprint races, but my Sibs prove themselves in the distance races. They have endurance, power and enough speed to be competitive in the sprint races, and I'm also finding that the Siberian people (and there are a *lot* of us) just compete among ourselves in these races. My team can average 18 to 22 miles per hour in a training run. That is fast enough for me. The *very fast* teams sometimes attain speeds of 28 to 30. You can

An Alaskan Husky in the foreground and a Siberian Husky sitting in the background.

Another Alaskan Husky. Note the broad, deep chest, wide set legs, and slender body. He has blue eyes, a common characteristic of the Siberian Husky, and cream-colored hair with dark brown markings. You can tell by his muscled body that he's in fantastic shape.

A hound-mix. Notice the long slender legs and streamlined body. His back legs have great angulation, with long pasterns and toes. This dog looks like he can run like a rabbit.

see why the dogs need to have a slender body and long legs. Whipping through trees at this speed on a four foot wide trail, also requires a few prayers. I've hit my share of trees and even at 18 to 22 miles per hour it's a sudden stop.

While Nordic-type dogs may be a little slower, they are still very competitive. These breeds have a more muscular body and a wide, deep-set chest giving them larger lung capacity and greater endurance. These breeds also have a shorter, stockier leg and their feet are usually tougher.

If you were to compare a hound-mix and a Siberian Husky and stand them side by side, you would find the hound has a narrower chest. He also has longer legs, which give the appearance that he is able to jump an eight-foot fence from a stand-still. His coat is thin and short, the hindquarters usually drop slightly, and his feet are splayed with longer toes than the Husky. The hound-mix comes in assorted colors due to the mixture of various breeds.

The Siberian has a much heavier double coat. His toes are closer together, as the foot is more tightly compressed so the snow does not pack between the snug toes when working in the cold Nordic conditions. The hair on the foot is short and the feet are tough. All these characteristics make for a more efficient foot.

LEGS AND SHOULDERS

The legs of a sled dog must be strong with good angular projection. The shoulder blade should be well laid back at an approximate angle of 45-degrees to the ground. The muscles should be tight and firm. Ideally, the angle formed by the shoulder blade and upper arm is about 90 degrees. This allows maximum shock absorbency when the dog is running, while the 45-degree set of the shoulder allows maximum reach and follow through.

There should be a slight slant to the pasterns, with the pastern joint strong and flexible, and the legs should not be too heavy.

The hind legs should be moderately spaced and straight from the point of the hip to the ground. The stifles should be well bent and the hock joint well defined and set low to the ground to give the dog thrust or drive.

THE FEET OF SLED DOGS

The shape of the foot is very important. The toes of the Nordic dogs are tight together. The toes should be well arched so that the soft part of the pad is up off the snow. If the toes are splayed, the toenails can be easily pulled and snow and ice can pack up in the soft area of the foot and cause pain.

Some dogs won't let you know they are in pain until they can hardly walk, let alone run. They are so into their running that you have to be the one to watch for any signs of trouble. There have been times I have pulled snowballs from my dogs' feet that were as big as golf balls and they could hardly walk. One sign to watch for: every time you stop or slow down the dog will stop and start to chew on his foot. He probably has a snowball or some ice caught up in his foot. If you see a little blood on the trail, he may have pulled a toenail. Stop and check.

The hound or hunting dog's feet are usually splayed and sometimes webbed with a fan of skin between the toes for swimming. When going through brush, tulles, and dry land, feet that are splayed allow the foot and long toes to flow over these obstacles better. However, this same foot on ice and snow can be hazardous. A dog with long, splayed toes, if pulling

Notice the proper angulation of the hind quarters and the
front legs and how the hind legs are angled back, giving the
dog great thrust.

The foot of a Siberian Husky. Note
the compactness, with short hair
and short nails.

You can see how snow can easily
gather between the toes of these
splayed feet and cause a problem.

THE IDEAL SLED DOG

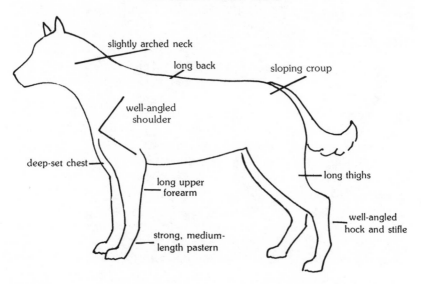

This is a drawing of what I believe a running dog should be built like. It will give you some idea of what is best suited for running and pulling a sled.

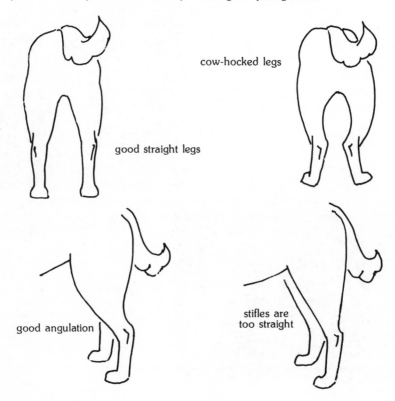

extremely hard, can actually break toes. The hound type foot also has some advantages—it can really dig into soft snow for that fast pace.

THE COAT

When choosing your sled dog keep in mind the length of his coat. Long-haired dogs can be run just like short-haired dogs, however, their coats will need a lot more care. The hair must be trimmed around the dog's legs, under his stomach and on the hind legs. If the hair is long and the weather is warm the dog can become overheated. Feet can become a problem if long hairs are not clipped from between the toes. The snow will stick more on softer haired than on coarser haired dogs. Collies and Irish Setters are two breeds with soft hair that can collect snowballs. The Malamute's coat is coarser, but can also collect snow when he becomes too warm.

The Siberian Husky, Samoyed, Norwegian Elkhound, Chow, Eskimo Dog, Alaskan Malamute and Great Pyrenees are among the breeds that have double coats. This means they have an undercoat of fine fur beneath a longer top coat. This type of coat keeps the Nordic dog warm in sub-zero temperatures. They thrive when it is 10° F. They will curl up with their tail wrapped around their face and can withstand a horrendous blizzard without any shelter. But remember that while the cold feels so good to them, warm weather can cause them to collapse on the trail from overheating.

Once while I was running a middle distance race, one of my longer haired dogs, Zak, overheated and went down on me. He was a Siberian Husky with a very thick, black coat. I had to pick him up and put him into my dog-bag and carry him in the sled the last ten miles of the race. Zak weighs about sixty pounds, and with the trail as steep as it was, it was a great deal of work for me as well as the rest of the team. At the time I didn't know he could have died from heat prostration. To quickly lower his body temperature, I should have stopped and packed his head in snow. We were lucky . . . Zak survived the ordeal. Some dogs do not.

In regard to the single-coated dog, the opposite is true. Care must be taken so he does not get too cold after a run. I've seen some of the hound mix breeds sit and shiver until they are put away in their dog boxes. Since they cool down more quickly than double coated dogs, they should be crated sooner after a race or workout.

3
The Strength
of the Sled Dog

Have you ever seen a team of dogs running down a snow-packed trail? It looks like they aren't pulling any weight at all; they just effortlessly glide along. But in fact some of those dogs are pulling as much as 200 pounds, depending on how much the driver and the sled weighs. These dogs are strong!

The Nordic breeds especially are noted for their incredible strength, and I have heard it stated that the Siberian Husky is the strongest animal for its size in the world.

Contests to see who has the strongest dog have become popular. Some of the drivers use their dogs for sprint races and in between the sprint races enter them in pulling contests. The average sled dog should be able to easily pull his own weight. A sled weighs around 30 to 35 pounds and glides easily once in motion. Once trained, the dog should be able to pull you and the sled with ease. You may have to help once in a while when a hill is encountered, but that's part of running dogs. Even with a big team, you end up running a lot. To keep a steady pace up and down hills, you have to work hard, too.

When you begin training your dog to pull, start with something light-weight like a small log weighing around five pounds. The idea is to get him used to something dragging behind him. Then gradually increase the weight when he can pull that amount easily. If you are starting out with a puppy, start slowly. I start my pups at three months with a ten-inch piece of 2x4. You want this to be *fun* for the dog. You do not want the little harness to choke him or the weight so heavy that he has to struggle to run. If your puppy is really small and a ten-inch piece of wood is too large, use a smaller one. By the time he is six months old he should be able to pull twenty pounds with ease.

The reason we teach a dog to pull with weights is to enable him to continue pulling without breaking stride when encountering a hill or deep snow. He has to be able to *pull* the sled and not be thinking about it, just running in a good steady lope. While the puppy or adult dog is being trained to pull, he is developing the muscles he will need for running. He learns to pull with his front feet and drive with his hind legs. When a dog is trained slowly and carefully he will enjoy pulling and not hurt himself. It is the same process used by human weight lifters, who can injure themselves by lifting weights too soon and too often. A puppy should be worked for about five or ten minutes every day with a lot of loving and play added.

When starting with an adult dog, use the same procedure. This dog could probably pull a lot of weight, but start him off slowly anyway. If you rush him, he may never pull. In the chapters to follow I will explain *how* to train your dog to pull with weights, how to harness the dog, and all the equipment needed to get him to the starting line of your first race.

Any dog can be trained to pull as long as it's done properly. I've seen small dogs weighing no more than 35 pounds pull as much weight as some of the big dogs weighing 60 pounds. However, if you plan to train for weight pulling, consider the larger, well muscled breeds like Mastiff or Malamute, or maybe even St. Bernard. Just remember, no matter what type of dog, go slowly, let him get the feel of it, and make it *fun for him!*

COMPETITIVE WEIGHT PULLING

There are weight-pulling contests all over the country. This competition involves a dog's ability to pull tremendous weight on a sled within a given time and distance. The sled is usually a flat bed on runners and is piled high with dog food bags or cement bricks. If the sponsor of the race is a dog food company, then dog food is used, as it is already marked for weight and is easy to arrange the proper weight. The distance is usually 16 feet, with the chute being around 10 feet wide. Snow fencing is used to divide the chutes being used and two or three contests can be run one right after the other.

The dog can be encouraged by his trainer but not touched. He wears a special freight harness which distributes the weight evenly across his body to the sled or cart (carts are used when there is no snow). The weight of the dog determines his class. There are usually four classes: Under 50

Pounds; 50 to 80 Pounds; 81 to 110 Pounds; Unlimited Pounds. The following table lists the results of the Championship Weight-Pulling contests in 1984. The competition was in Billings, Montana, with a purse of $2,000.

50 Pound/Under Class	Dog's Wt.	Lbs. Pulled	Sec.
1. Max/Bob LeCour	46.5	588.5	9.6
2. Cinnamon/Mike Doolin	46.0	488.5	9.0
3. Kasha/Lew Hicks	43.25	438.5	12.2

In 1986, Sam, owned by Dave Larson of Laurel, Montana, set a record when he pulled 3,130 pounds a distance of 16 feet in 9.23 seconds. Sam is a beautiful Golden Mastiff.

At this same contest an Alaskan Husky named Mars, owned by Tom Fink, won the 60 Pound Class Under, shattering his own record of 1,570 pounds with a pull of 2,080 pounds. These dogs compete in an elimination competition by attempting to pull increasing amounts of weight on a sled over a snow-packed surface. They pull the sled in a 16 foot chute within a one minute time frame. There was a $6,000 purse at this pull. A lot of people are getting interested in the pulling contests because you need only one dog to participate and, as you can see, there is some impressive prize money.

"SAM", an incredible Mastiff, has set the record for weight-pulling—3,130 pounds, sixteen feet, in 9.23 seconds. The dog is all muscle and sloppy kisses.

This little dog was in the 60 Pound/Under Class. You can see how he strains into the harness to pull the weight. The first line in the foreground is the sixteen-foot marker; the cart has to cross this line and the dog the second line.

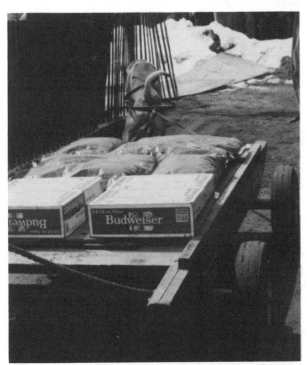

This wheeled cart is used on a smooth surface. Note the wooden dowel under the dog's tail as he is pulling. This keeps the webbed harness from rubbing on the dog's thigh.

4
Introduction to Dog Sled Equipment

Anyone can run a team of sled dogs, or even one dog, and have great fun going it. Some basic equipment is needed to get started. It is important to have the right equipment, some of which you will be able to make yourself, and some will have to be purchased. (See appendix for a list of Outfitters where equipment can be purchased.)

I started out with all homemade equipment, because I didn't know where to purchase it. In doing this I had harnesses that didn't fit properly and ganglines that were too short.

The type of equipment you need will depend somewhat on the area of the country you live in. In a warm climate where it seldom snows, you could use a cart instead of a sled. If there is snow during the winter, you could use a cart for training in the late fall and a sled when the snows come.

There are several ways to have your dog pull you—try skis using a long rope attached to the dog's harness; one of those little sleds on which the kids go screaming down the hills; a lightweight three-wheeled cart; or even an ATV (all terrain vehicle). Finally, there is a well-crafted dog sled. After your dog has been trained to pull, he can even bring in the small logs you've cut for firewood or the perfect Christmas tree you couldn't locate from your vehicle.

HARNESSES AND THEIR HISTORY

A harness is the gear a dog wears for pulling. The harness goes around the dog's neck and over his back as illustrated. The main line, which is hooked to whatever the dog is pulling, is then hooked to the loop that is near the dog's tail. This enables the dog to pull the object in tow.

No one really knows when the first dogs were harnessed and used to pull cargo or what type of harnesses were used. In the early 1800's harnesses consisted of leather thongs tied around the dog's neck with a long lead from this collar to the object in tow. At that time the Eskimos used a "fan" hitch, where several dogs were hooked to one point and allowed to pull freely. They didn't use leaders that would lead out a single line of dogs, as this fan of dogs made sense with the wide open spaces of the Arctic ice to run on. Later, dogs were harnessed in two straight rows with one line going between the dogs—one on each side in pairs—or in single file with the line hooked to the collar and the back of the harness. The dogs were hooked to this line by ropes, called tuglines, attached to the main line. This tugline was hooked to a leather harness, something like our present day tracking harness. This freighting-type harness, used in the early days for pulling heavy freight sledges, was made of a rather heavy leather. It had a strap, like a collar, that went around the dog's neck and buckled. A strap on each side of this collar connected it to yet another strap that went around the dog's stomach and was buckled in place. This way the driver could *fit* the harness to each dog. One size fit all, so to speak. The dogs were placed single file, and the two main lines (ganglines) rested on the outside of the dogs and snapped onto the band around the stomach. Sometimes as many as twenty dogs were used in a line to pull heavy sledges. The frequently used trails were narrow and deep from many dogs and heavy sledges that passed over them.

Now racers use a lighter-weight, more efficient harness and an easier way to hook the dogs into a gangline. The new harnesses are made from a colorful light-weight nylon-webbed material. This flat-webbed material lies close to the dog's body, allowing optimum transfer of strength from dog to sled. This gives the dog the best advantage to pull his load.

A dog left alone for a time could devour a leather harness in a short time. As you know, a dog loves to eat leather. There is less chance of a dog chewing the nylon harness. However, I still lose a few each year. There is a product called *Bitter Apple* that will deter chewing but needs to be used often. You get this product at pet stores and it is inexpensive.

DIFFERENT TYPES OF HARNESSES

Three or four standard harness designs are being used today. There is the *cross-backed racing harness*, a *light-weight race harness;* the *weight-pulling harness;* and the *freight harness*, which is similar to the weight pulling harness. Some freight harnesses are still made from leather but they are hard to come by.

The most popular is the *cross-backed RACING HARNESS*. This harness is non-restrictive harness made for maximum comfort with optimum transfer of strength from dog to sled. With the extra interlacement of material, the harness lays flat on the dog's back not allowing the harness to slip off to one side. This harness is also used for cross-country *ski-joring* (hooking a dog to a long line and letting him pull you on skis). It should fit closely to the dog's body, snug around his neck, and should end with the loop for the tugline at the dog's tail. The neck opening should fit snugly but not so tight that you cannot get his collar through the opening. The collar must come through the opening and lay on top of the harness so hooking the neck line on the gangline won't cause the collar to pull the harness to one side and choke the dog. The harness has a soft pile material around the neck opening and under the chest to protect the dog from the constant jolting of the tuglines and the sudden stops when braking.

Notice how this weight-pulling harness fits, distributing the weight low, alongside of the dog. Note the wooden dowel at the tail.

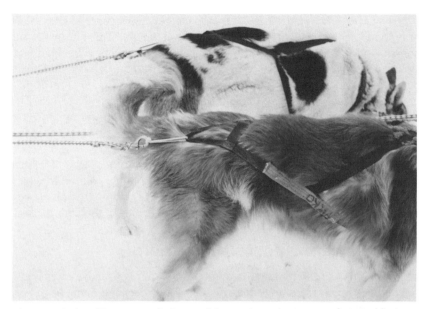

A correctly-fitted harness with the small loop where the tugs are fastened laying just in front of the dog's tail.

Neversummer® sled dog outfitters has just come up with a new *CROSS-COUNTRY* harness which is just like the cross-backed race harness, except it has padding around the neck and down the front which extends under the dog's legs and up past the rib-cage. This gives extra protection for the long distance races; and pieces of reflector tape across the dog's back allow your team to be seen with a headlamp at night. These are great harnesses for the everyday driver, too, because you can see your dogs during a snow storm and when training at night. The extra padding is more comfortable for the dogs.

The *LIGHT-WEIGHT RACE HARNESS* is made from single-webbed nylon braiding. It does not have the extra cross-piece along the dog's back. While this harness is quite a bit cheaper in cost, it has its draw backs. The harness slips when the dog is pulling into it and can chafe the dog during long trips. The material can twist and tangle. It has padding around the neck opening and down the front just as the cross-backed harness.

The *WEIGHT-PULLING HARNESS* is usually a cross-backed type similar to the race harness, but constructed for pulling heavy loads. It is non-restrictive cross-backed design with a wooden spreader-bar in the rear. It lays across the dog's back like the racing harness, but it hangs lower on the side so the direction of pull is below that of the racing harness. This lowers the center of gravity and increases the dog's stability and strength while pulling in the heaviest competitions. This harness may also be made from tubular nylon for added strength.

The *FREIGHT HARNESS* is usually leather; however, it can be made of nylon which is less expensive and lighter in weight. This harness is still constructed just as it was a hundred years ago. The collar is buckled with straps running from the collar to the belly band. Both neck piece and belly-band are padded. There are rings on the belly-band where the double gangline is attached. Dogs in freight harnesses are placed single-file. The pull is on the side of the dog as with the weight-pulling harness.

Another version of this harness has the wooden spreader-bar at the back like the weight-pulling harness, but in this case the tugline is attached at the end of the harness. A small piece of rope or another piece of leather goes from each side of the spreader-bar to a ring in the middle to which the tugline is attached. Either a double hook-up or two dogs running side by side can be used with this type of harness. A single gangline is used.

HOW A HARNESS SHOULD FIT THE DOG

When measuring for a harness, remember to measure the dog's body, not his hair. Since some dogs have heavy winter coats and many have long hair, you need to list the breed when ordering your harness. The harness is designed to lay flat on the dog's back, go between the dog's front legs and ride across the last rib. The end of the harness should end up at the dog's tail where the tugline is connected. The chest strap should be rather wide and have good padding. It should not choke the dog or cause undo pressure on the breastbone. The chest strap should come down between the dog's front legs, separate just behind the elbow and run upward to the tail (not beyond it). If the harness fits too loosely on the dog, it will cause him to have an uneven pull and he will compensate by running sideways and not tracking properly. An improper fit also can cause discomfort and strain, pain in the chest area, and can rub off hair—like wearing a pair of shoes that doesn't fit quite right.

The sample order sheet shows how to measure your dog for a harness. Take the time to do it carefully as this is one of the most important pieces of equipment needed for training your dog and he cannot work well without a correctly fitted harness.

HOW TO PUT A HARNESS ON YOUR DOG

The first time you put on the harness it may frighten your dog, so let him smell it and get acquainted with it before you begin. Make this whole procedure as much fun as you can; never let him become frightened of the harness. Some dogs become so excited when they see the harness it is almost impossible to harness them. I usually stand over the dog and clamp my legs around his middle to get a better hold.

HOW TO ORDER A HARNESS

This diagram will show you how to order a harness, remembering to measure close to the dog's body, not on top of the hair. The harness should fit snugly. Measure around the neck just ahead of the withers (point A) to the top of the breastbone (point B) and back around to point A. To get the length, measure from top of the breastbone (point B), down the chest, between the front legs, passing under the dog, then up around the last rib to the base of tail (point C). Then measure from point A to the last rib (point D). The last measurement will be from point B to point D. The breed should also be mentioned to the outfitter so he can compensate for hair and body structure. Also the weight and age of the dog should be stated.

Make sure dog is standing square and solid.

1. NECK (A-B-A)   _____
2. LENGTH (B-C)   _____
3. A to B   _____
4. B to D   _____
5. WEIGHT   _____
6. AGE   _____
7. BREED   _____

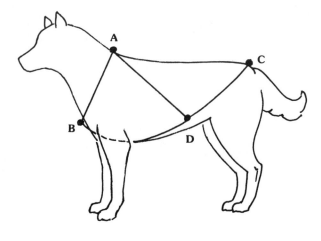

Pick up the harness, holding it on each side of the neck opening, then pick up each side of the harness that goes under the dog's front legs. Now you are ready to put it over the dog's head. Make sure the piece going down the dog's chest is pointing away from you. Slip the harness over the dog's head, pull it over his collar, then lift the collar over the harness so it rides freely. Pull one side down across the dog's back and put his leg through the leg opening. Lift the leg gently, bend the leg at the knee making it easier to put the leg through the opening. Pull the other side down; put the other leg through the leg opening and straighten the harness across the dog's back. The loop should be at his tail. Pull the hair up a little at the neck opening so it doesn't get caught in the harness. Make sure there aren't any twisted areas.

If you are only running one dog, the line running to the object in tow will be attached directly to the loop at the end of the harness. If you are running a team of three or more the gangline will run between the dogs and they will be hooked to the collar by the neckline and to the harness by the tugline.

GANGLINES

When the first expeditions went to the Arctic they found the natives driving dogs with long leather leashes attached to their collars. These leashes were attached to a sled made from the antlers of Reindeer or whalebone. The sledges where awkward and heavy and the dogs were spread out in

Step One: Pick up the harness, hold it on either side of the neck opening, then pick up each side of the harness that goes under the dog's front legs. The long chest-piece will stick out in front and should be facing away from you at this point. Slip the harness over the dog's head. Pull the collar up through the opening until it is on top of the harness. Adjust the dog's hair so it isn't being pulled.

Step Two: Now take the right leg and pull it through the leg opening, pull the harness down across the dog's back. Make sure the harness isn't twisted.

Step Three: Pull the left leg through the leg opening and stretch the harness to its fullest down to the tail.

Now your dog is harnessed; the loop should come to the dog's tail.

what is called a *fan hitch*. They didn't have leaders to lead the teams, nor did they have trails to follow on the hard, barren ice. There were a lot of dog fights and the dogs were very hard to control. At this time the Eskimos were using wolves mixed with their village dogs. Eventually someone discovered a better way to hook up the dogs so they could not only pull more evenly but could be controlled easier. The gangline evolved.

The gangline is a line that runs between the dogs and the object in tow. This rope is connected to each dog by one small rope connecting the collar and one connecting the harness. The gangline is the means of pulling the sled; there is no line from the dogs to the driver, so the dogs must be commanded by voice, without any restraint.

The gangline is usually made from three-eights polyethylene rope. It comes in green and white, blue and white, or red and white diamond braid. The length of this line is determined by the number of dogs being run. The necklines coming off the main gangline are made of a lighter-weight, one-quarter inch polyethylene rope. The tugline that connects the harness to the gangline is usually one-quarter or three-eights-inch poly rope. There is one neckline and one tugline per dog. If there is a double or two dogs running side by side, there will be two necklines and two tuglines, one for each dog in that position. The two lead dogs will have only tuglines connected to the gangline, and a single piece of poly rope with a snap at either end attached to their collars keeps them running side by side.

NECKLINES

The neckline, ten to twelve inches long with a snap at the end, keeps the dog going in a forward direction along the gangline. When the dog is standing with the tugline snug, the neckline should be directly in line with the dog's collar. The dog should not have to be stretched to fasten the neckline in place.

TUGLINES

The tugline connecting the harness to the gangline is approximately thirty-six to forty-two inches long, depending upon the type of dogs. Siberian Huskies and the Nordic breeds need to have more freedom and will need a longer tugline and more space between them. The hounds run in packs and therefore can be run closer together with a little shorter tugline. However, the tugline should never be shorter than thirty-six inches. A five-eights-inch brass snap fastens the end of the tugline to the harness.

SAFETY LINE

You should have an extra line coming off the main gangline to the sled or cart as a safety-line. This will give you a second chance if the main

GANGLINE HITCHES

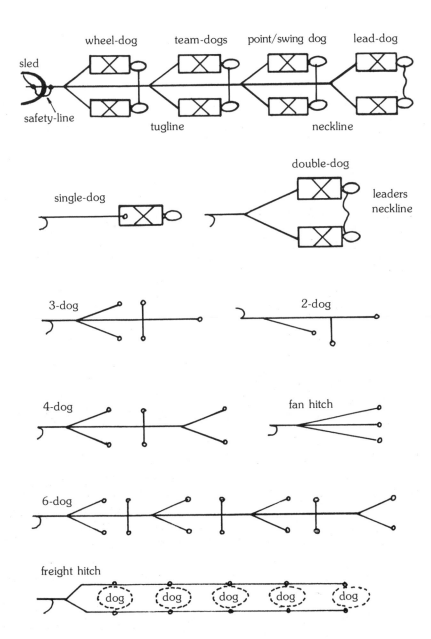

snap breaks. This line can be twelve to fourteen inches long and is just an extension of the main gangline. If it weren't for the safety-line I was using once I would have lost my team and had a long walk trying to find them. The main snap didn't close properly and came loose. I had a friend in the sled with me and would have been quite embarrassed if the dogs took off without us. I kept quiet until I could stop and fix it, smiled as if nothing were wrong, and we took off again very thankful for such small things as a safety-line.

Different Types of Gangline Hitches

The type of gangline hitch you choose will depend on how many dogs you will be running and on individual choice. Some of the most common hitches are illustrated. You can make a single-dog gangline (where dogs are run in single-file) and hook as many dogs single-file as you want, or you can use a double hook-up. If you have made a double hookup gangline and are running six dogs and one has a problem, you can put that dog in the sled and hook the extra tug and neckline to the dog next to the one you took out. There are approximately eight feet between each set of dogs, so if you run ten dogs in a single line, you would have a long way to go to get to the leader. It would be better to run five dogs in a double hitch or five in a six-dog hitch, four double plus a single leader. In this case you would hook both tuglines to the lead dog's harness.

When choosing your gangline remember to use brass snaps instead of plated snaps. Brass snaps are much stronger and will not break as easy

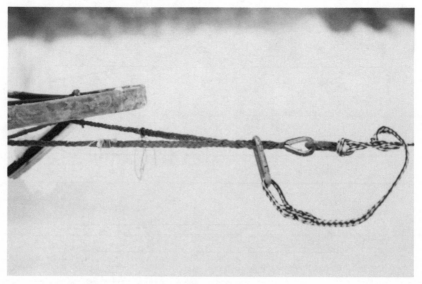

The sled with the safety and ganglines attached.

28

in sub-zero temperatures, and they can be opened when frozen by rubbing or blowing on them.

There are many ways to hook up a team and it will, of course, depend on how many dogs you're running. Running them in pairs gives the dogs more confidence and will usually work better in the beginning. Using a double lead will definitely give the leaders more confidence. However, some dogs do not like to be hooked side by side and you may have to run them singly. There are leaders who like to run alone and do very well. They are usually very confident and take commands well. Often they were trained alone.

Attaching the Gangline

On a sled is a rope that is attached to the stanchion on one side, runs under the brush-bow and across to the other side. The gangline hooks into a loop in the center of this line. This is called the sled's bridle. To help absorb the shock from the gangline, a bungie cord is usually inserted into the bridle or into the gangline itself. The stopping and starting of a sled or cart causes a great deal of jerking.

On a cart, there is a metal loop in which to hook the gangline and the safety line. On this type of hookup you can hook a bungie cord to the steel ring and then into the gangline to absorb the shock. I usually use one of the flat black bungie cords. Make sure the "S" hooks are bent so they can't come loose.

To attach the gangline to the cart, snap the gangline and the safety line to the loop provided for this at the front of the cart. Be sure to use a bungie cord to help absorb the shock from the bouncing and jerking of the cart. Notice the large spring on top of the front wheel which helps to absorb some of the shock when traveling down a bumpy dirt road.

5
Carts and Wheeled Rigs

The wheeled rig or cart can be used in some of the warmer areas year round. It is also used for early fall training before the snows come. A cart is a lot of fun and the whole family can join in or you can give company a ride when they come to visit. In some areas the cart is used for racing instead of a sled. The cart is light enough that two or three dogs can pull it easily, thus making it a popular vehicle for pet owners.

There are many ways to build a cart. Some drivers use the rear-axle, of a small car and build a steel framework with a single or double wheel in the front. The cart has to be strong, with good suspension and a low center of gravity. There should be some sort of shock absorption to help with the constant jolting and vibration.

The carts shown here were built by professional sled and cart builders. From these you can perhaps get your own ideas. Remember, the cart must be heavy enough so you have some control over the dogs when you stop them, and it *must* have a holding brake, some way to contain the team when you stop, or they will simply run off with your cart. I've run after my team more than once because the team was too strong for the light-weight cart I was using.

1. Brake
2. Steering Bar
3. Braking Plate
4. Standing Platform
5. Steering Rod
6. Gangline Hook-up
7. Swivel Wheel
8. Collapsible Braces (allows
   the cart to be lowered to
   wheel height for traveling.)

The cart or wheeled rig is made from steel bars or tubing. It is designed to withstand the constant vibration and jarring from the dirt roads and trails. It has a heavy spring on the front wheel and is considered a light-weight cart.

HEAVY CART

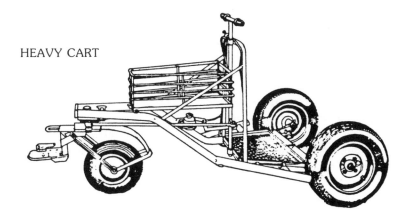

This cart is the heaviest cart of the two models. It has a steel basket for gear and a trailer hitch for pulling it with a vehicle. It also has a much stronger braking system on it. This cart could handle eight to ten dogs.

THE LIGHT-WEIGHT CART

This cart, built by Frank Hall, weighs about one hundred pounds. On a flat surface one or two dogs can pull it easily, but no more than five or six dogs should be run at a time with it. The braking system will not hold a large team, and the cart, being light-weight, will be dragged.

The Steering

The cart is steered by a rod coming from the front wheel, which is welded onto another rod running the length of the cart and mounted to the handle brace. A piece of smaller pipe with a cross-bar on it for a steering wheel is bolted to this rod. When the steering bar is moved, it, in turn, moves the rod that is attached to the front wheel. The front wheel is on a swivel and has a heavy spring to absorb some of the shock. This cart can be turned sharply when negotiating turns. On heavier carts the steering mechanism and also the rear-end from a small car is sometimes used.

The Braking System

On the light-weight cart, the braking mechanism is a rod going to each wheel with a steel plate that presses against the tires when the brake is applied. This brake can be locked in place and used for an emergency brake, but is not strong enough for a large team. The brake is applied using a foot peddle in front of the platform, leaving your hands free to steer. When the brake is applied lightly, it will slow the team down and when it is pressed all the way forward, it locks.

On a heavier cart the system is more elaborate using hydraulic pressure to stop the cart. A foot peddle in front of the platform operates this device. It is the same system used on golf carts. Even though it has hydraulic-braking system, and the cart could weigh as much as 200 pounds, a strong team can still pull the cart with the wheels locked down the road with or without you, so be careful. Don't ever leave the cart unattended unless you tie it to a tree or have someone helping you.

You must use caution when driving a cart as they can tip over and you can get hurt if you are turning too sharply or going too fast. However, most carts have a low center of gravity and are balanced quite well.

You can run the dogs as long as it is not too hot. If the temperature is below 60°F they can run for a couple miles, or run at night when it cools off. Rig up some running lights or have someone drive behind with a car. This gives some added protection if you are on a public road. It's pretty hard to see a team of dogs and a cart at night.

Most serious sled drivers have a cart for training because it gets the dogs conditioned early in the fall and ready for the sled by the time the snow comes. The light-weight cart shown in these illustrations can have the braces unscrewed and the sides let down so it can be transported easily in the back of a pickup truck to a place where it is safe to run the dogs.

After your team is trained you might want to organize a cart race at the local fairgrounds (if it has a track). In some states they race on country roads or on circular tracks. Limit the size of the teams to keep the sport safe. All in all, driving a cart is a sport all of its own. I enjoy driving a cart because it's fast, bumpy (you feel like your eye-balls are going to jiggle out of your head at times), and thrilling as you make fast turns, bending down to keep a low center of gravity. Use your imagination and have fun with your dogs — you'll be surprised how much they love it.

The brake is a simple device. When the peddle is pushed forward, it will cause the brake-plates to press against the wheels. When the peddle is pressed farther forward it will lock in place. To release this locked position, press a little farther forward and the end will lift up and release the brake. You can see the plates clamped against the wheels; you can also see how the steering rod is attached to the steering handle.

6
Sleds

There are many sleds used today, some home-made from old skis and slats put together to form a reasonable facsimile, others made from high-tech plastic, and still others made from hardwood like birch or white ash by professional sled builders. The art of sled building is quite a unique craft. The sled has to be very strong, yet light in weight. Hardwoods can be bent to shape the runners, brushbow, and handlebow (see illustration).

Many years ago in Alaska, freight sledges were used as I've mentioned before. The original freighting sledges weighed as much as 300 pounds (empty) and 1500 pounds when loaded. These sleds had wire wrapped with rawhide as reinforcement between the stanchions and thick runners covered with steel. The basket went from the brushbow to the handlebow. Sledges were hard to turn; the driver had to throw all his weight to the outside and pull hard to turn them with their great loads. Sometimes a long pole was used to help push the sled around.

In recent years, sleds have become much lighter and shorter. They weigh less than thirty-five pounds and can take turns easily at thirty miles per hour.

There are still three basic sled types: The sprint (racing) sled, the toboggan sled (used for long distance races like the Iditarod in Alaska), and the freight sled.

THE LIGHT-WEIGHT SPRINT SLED

This sled can be a bolted sled with screws holding the joints together or a hand-tied rawhide-laced sled. The rawhide sled sometimes has bolted joints to give it added strength. Some have rawhide wrapped around the handlebow and the brushbow for added strength. Most racers prefer plastic runners because they are faster and the snow doesn't stick to them unless it is very cold. Of course, one can rub ski wax onto the runners to make the sled go faster.

This conventional bolted racing sled without any rawhide lacing or wrapped brushbow is the cheapest type of sled. This is a good sled for the beginner. This one was built by Frank Hall and is considered the "economy sled."

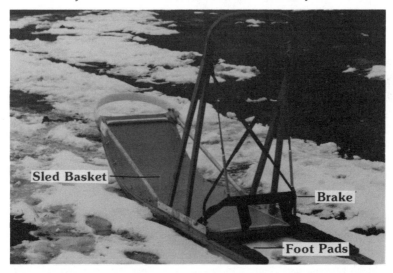

This is the toboggan sled used in the Alaskan Iditarod. The sled can hold up to 300 pounds of equipment and has a nylon bag which is bolted onto the back stanchion and right at the brushbow. The bag ties near the top of the handlebow and usually has a long zipper or ties the length of the bag. A driver will carry equipment and sometimes an injured dog here.

THE TOBOGGAN SLED

The toboggan sled is used in sprint racing as well in long- distance races. Built close to the ground with the basket riding on the runners, this sled has a very low center of gravity and does not tip over easily. When it does, it will usually bounce back. These sleds are a little heavier than the race sled because of the full plastic basket and heavier runners. The toboggan seems to float over the snow, is very easy to ride, and corners well. The runners in the back where you stand are short, but the basket is long, so the over-all sled is about the same length as the racing sled. I really like this type because you can carry more on it. It weighs forty-five to fifty pounds, depending on how it is made.

THE FREIGHT SLED

The freight sled is still being used in some areas for touring, which has become a big industry for the ski resorts and snow country. Dan MacEachen of Aspen, Colorado, uses twelve to sixteen dogs to pull a heavy sled to take people on dog sledding trips. Another young man in Steamboat Springs hauls out big game during the elk and bear hunting season.

A freight sled. Notice the width of the runners and sturdiness of this sled. You can see how it can haul heavy loads. It has twisted rawhide to strengthen the stanchions. The brush and handlebows are both wrapped with rawhide for greater support, as is the first stanchion closest to the brushbow. Remember, when going over moguls, or over logs on the trail, the front of the sled will take the brunt of the shock, especially with a heavy load. Note also the short runner where the driver stands. On pleasure sleds they are much longer allowing for faster turns.

Photo courtesy of Dan MacEachen, Aspen, Colorado

WHERE'S THE BEEF? AND PARTS ARE PARTS!

The "beef" of a dog sled is the *brushbow*, the circular extension in front of the sled. This brace protects the sled and is the first part of the sled to hit an oncoming object (such as a tree), so it has to be very strong. Some drivers wrap their brushbow with rawhide or tape it with duct tape. I've even seen a sled with nylon string wrapped tightly around the brushbow. Rawhide is put on wet, then laced in place. When it dries it's incredibly strong. I've glanced off of trees at speeds of twenty miles per hour and done little, if any, damage to the sled. Once I hit a tree so hard that when the sled hit the tree it wedged between the brushbow and the gangline. I flew over the sled into a snow bank. Yes, it was indeed a sudden stop! The dogs could have been injured seriously but a good harness saved them from possible fractured collar bones. And all it did to my sled was put a small hole in the rawhide.

These things do happen—it's just part of sledding. Frank Hall once told me, "You aren't a real musher until you've dumped and and lost your sled at least twelve times."

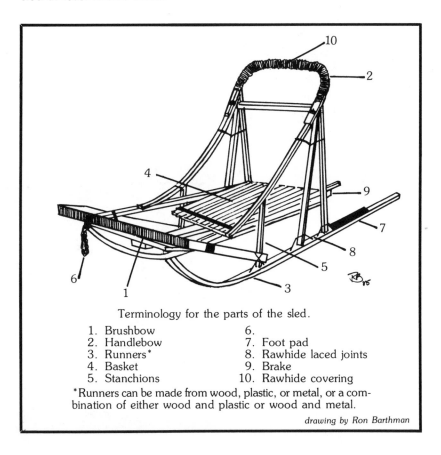

Terminology for the parts of the sled.

1. Brushbow
2. Handlebow
3. Runners*
4. Basket
5. Stanchions

6.
7. Foot pad
8. Rawhide laced joints
9. Brake
10. Rawhide covering

*Runners can be made from wood, plastic, or metal, or a combination of either wood and plastic or wood and metal.

drawing by Ron Barthman

THE BASKET

The basket is necessary for many reasons. The snow hook is carried here, and if a dog is injured, he must be put into a dog-bag and carried in the basket. There are half-baskets and full-baskets. The slats are 1x½-inch and run the length of the basket, bolted or laced with rawhide to the main frame. They are strong enough to allow passengers to ride when necessary.

A beautifully crafted sled. The hours it takes to build a sled like this are what the drivers pay for—sleds are not cheap.

Some of the sleds are lashed together both at the runners and at the basket.

38

HANDLEBOW

The handle or driving bow steers the sled. The handlebow is made of wood wrapped with rawhide, tape, or thin nylon string; or it can be made from plastic, which is wrapped to keep your hands from slipping when it's grabbed in a hurry (the handle is often wet from snow).

By twisting the handlebow and slightly picking up the front of the sled, you can put the runners on their edges just like a pair of skis to make sharp turns. Some sleds like Frank Hall's "Pro-Race Sled" have a swivel action to them. By simply applying pressure to one side or the other, you can put the runners on their edges, making it easier to corner.

THE STANCHIONS

The stanchions of a sled are the framework. These can be either bolted or laced with rawhide or nylon string, or both. If you have bolted stanchions on your sled be sure to check them often as the bolts work loose after awhile. If you have nylon or rawhide these also must be checked for wear. Sleds may have one, two or three stanchions, depending on how long the sled is and how it is designed.

THE RUNNERS

Runners are usually made of birch or ash, then covered with a layer of one-quarter or half-inch plastic or a thin strip of steel. However, there are sleds made with all plastic runners. Plastic bends easily when shaping the runner. Runners should have "built-in camber" to them. If you look at a ski, you will notice it gets a little narrower at the center of the ski, and if placed on a flat surface, the center of the ski is slightly raised off the hard

Notice how each piece of waxed string is laid flat and drawn tight. This sled, built by John Hensely, Leadville, Colorado, is rather stiff, but corners very well.

surface. This is called the camber of the ski. Mr. Hall puts this camber into the runners of his sled so that when turned on the edge, they will turn quickly. (Take a long, narrow piece of paper, hold both ends causing it to have a bend in the middle. Put this piece of paper on its side and see which way it would travel if it were in motion. It would bend right around and go the way the point is facing.)

When using plastic runners you must be very careful not to scratch them on sharp rocks or they will become marred and won't be as fast. Cold steel runners will be less likely to mar, but snow can stick to them when it gets very cold. The wise thing to do, I guess, would be to use cold rolled steel runners for training runs and screw on the plastic when the races start.

THE BRIDLE

The bridle, made from polyethlene rope, goes from the front two stanchions, under the brushbow, with a six-inch loop centered at the brushbow. There should be an eighteen to twenty-inch bungie cord inserted into the bridle to absorb the shock of the gangline. Insert the bungie cord, starting on one side. Push the poly rope together so you can insert the bungie, and keep pushing this cord all the way around to the other side, bypassing the loop for the gangline. Tie off both ends of the cord so it doesn't slip out of place (something like the old-fashioned Chinese finger snare).

FOOT PADS

We use bicycle tires cut to fit the area you want the foot-pad to go. Open them up and nail the sides along the runner and you have a non-slip pad to stand on. Grit pads (somewhat like sandpaper) maybe used but these wear out quickly and can pack with snow. There are times you have to guess where to step because the snow is so deep, but you get so used to standing at a certain distance with your feet apart that there is seldom a problem. The foot pad is placed just behind the last stanchion and is usually about twelve to fourteen inches long.

THE BRAKE

The brake consists of a piece of wood approximately two feet long attached to the center brace under the basket of the sled. It has a steel claw bolted at the end which, when stepped on, causes a drag on the sled. The brake goes down between the runners and is held up by a long spring. The dogs respond to this stopping action and should, with the command "whoa," come to a stop. As soon as you lift your foot off of the brake, the drag is released and the team is off and running again. A snow-hook is used for a more permanent tie-off. *NEVER leave your sled without securing it*, unless you just like to chase after your dogs!

This photo shows the bridle and how it is connected and the plastic runners along with the brake and how it is connected under the sled. You can also see how the brushbow is wrapped with rawhide.

Here you see how to wrap rawhide around the brushbow of the sled. Also, notice the bungie cord in the bridle. The poly-rope is thicker where the bungie cord is run through the rope. I have tied it off with string, and as you can see, I need to replace it soon.

The foot pads and braking system on a sled. The steel claw used for the brake is a very strong steel that won't bend with the beating it takes. As you can see, however, the points wear off with use.

This will give you some idea how the brake is attached to the bottom of the sled and how the bridle is run through the stanchions. Note the plastic runners. This sled has what is called a half basket. On some sleds, the basket is built all the way to the brushbow.

7
Snow Hooks
and Quick-Release

A snow hook is one item of importance you never want to leave behind when running dogs with a sled. It is the only means of securing a team without tying them off to a tree or fence, if you can find one. The snow hook is tied or snapped into the loop on the bridle with the gangline. Be sure to use a heavy snap. This way the dogs can pull against the snow hook instead of the sled. The hook is tied with a piece of poly or cotton rope to the bridle and run under the sled. It should be long enough to come to the foot pads on the runners or a little beyond so you can plant the snow hook right between your feet in a hurry if needed.

Some drivers with large teams use two snow hooks; one is used in the way I have just described and the second is snapped onto the wheel dogs. They use a three or four foot rope with a snap at the end and carry this extra snow hook in the sled, or they can use a longer rope and keep it snapped to the wheeler and, when they need it, unhook it from the carrier on the sled. Either way it's nice to have an extra hook along. One night some friends and I were training at a lake in Leadville and I was about to turn my six dog team around. As I put the hook down and set it, the dogs lunged and the snap broke on the line connecting the snow hook to the bridle. It was 10:30 at night and very dark. It was a relatively short run, only three miles and the team wasn't tired. It took me three-quarters of a mile before I could get the team stopped long enough to turn the leaders around. Times like this make you realize, "Maybe I should carry an extra snow hook!"

Some drivers prefer to pull the snow hook along side of the sled planting it on the outside of the runners where it is easily reached and isn't as likely to be pulled out of the snow by a runner. It is really personal preference as to *where* you set your hook. It also depends upon the snow conditions. In soft mushy snow the hook may not hold so you want it as close as possible in case you need to reset it in a hurry. When the snow is icy and hard, the problem is getting the hook out of the snow. Sometimes I have to drive my foot under the bar of the snow hook and lift it out with my foot, because the pressure being put against this hook by the team has *really* set it, so the hook must be in a position where I can do this without leaving the sled.

The snow hook is made of heavy steel bent at a ninety-degree angle. Many types of snow hooks are used, some homemade; others specially designed by a driver and hand crafted by professional iron workers.

To set the snow hook, as soon as the dogs stop and when applying the sled's brake, push the hook as deep into the snow as you can, then step on it and urge the team on slightly to make sure the hook is *set* and doesn't *give* when the team pulls. Sometimes you think the hook is set well only to find, after you have left the sled to go untangle a dog, that the hook has loosened and you get nailed by the sled as it goes barreling by. So setting the hook is very important. It is also very frustrating trying to loosen a snow hook that is buried deep into the crusted snow, but at least you still have your team.

You can use the snow hook to secure a team to a tree. Slow the team down, then stop them as close to a small tree (three or four-inches in diameter) as possible. Put your arm around the handlebow and drag the sled to the tree. Put the hook around the tree. If you plan to stay for any length of time, run a small line, perhaps an extra neckline with a snap at either end, around the tree and snap it onto the line again. Or, you can turn your sled on its side and then set the hook for extra protection.

ATTACHING THE SNOW HOOK TO THE SLED

The snow hook should be attached to the sled's bridle and not to one of the stanchions. If you attach the rope to the stanchions, the constant pulling of the dogs could break or weaken it. You will need a rope approximately six feet long with a large snap at one end. Tie the other end to the end of the snow hook. The snap fastens onto the loop on the bridle where you have snapped the gangline. Run the hook between the runners under the sled to just behind the foot pads where you stand. If the rope is too long, shorten it to the proper length. Pull the bridle taunt, the way the gangline will hold the bridle when the team is hooked up. Make sure the bridle is not pulled under the sled. Also make sure you can pull the hook up and

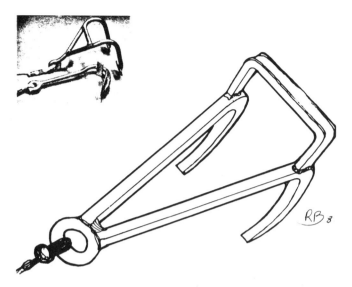

The snow hooks shown here are the basic snow hooks used in today's racing circuit. The larger snow hook in the foreground is the heavier of the three. This hook is one-inch steel bar and weighs bout seven pounds. The 'O' ring is used to tie the hook to the sled, and the cross-bar is the handle used to pull the hook from the snow. This hook will hold an eight-to-ten dog team. The other two snow hooks pictured are for a two- or three-dog team. They are light in weight and do not have the holding power the larger hook has. Snow hooks can be purchased at most outfitters.

Here you see approximately where to set the snow hook—just behind the foot pads on the runners. Notice the short rope on the cross-bar; this is used to pull the hook free when you want to release the hook.

over the back bar to put the hook into your sled's basket where you will be carrying it.

The hook is held in place by a bungie cord or by the dog bag (a bag used to carry an injured dog). You don't want the hook bouncing around when you are traveling. One man I know had five stitches in his eye because he dumped the sled and the hook came up and caught him in the face. So, be careful and make sure the hook is secured in the sled. Some drivers take a leather carpenter's pouch and attach it to the outside of the sled, which works well. You can put the hook into the pouch, back end first, and grab it quickly when you need it. Just be careful when you pass someone that it doesn't get caught on another driver's sled.

I ran a five-dog team for a year before I knew about snow hooks. I had all kinds of problems, and chased my team all over the country because I couldn't contain them to even turn them around.

You will learn to check your gear often for wear. The snaps and clips can wear out and come apart. Ropes can wear from the cold, dirt and sun beating constanly on them. Take a match and sear the frayed parts of poly rope.

THE QUICK-RELEASE

When you are ready to hook up a team to a sled or a cart you must secure the object in tow. If you have a fairly strong team and tie them using a slip knot, the dogs will pull it so tight you'll never get it loose. So the quick-release snap is used to release the dogs in a hurry. It is the same snap that is used for horse lead ropes. The specially designed snap will release no matter how much pressure is applied on the rope. You can use it to make a quick-release tether for your dog team.

The equipment you will need to make the quick-release can be purchased in any hardware or feed store where horse equipment is sold. You will need a quick-release snap and a 10-foot rope (cotton or poly or flat double-tubed nylon). I use three-eighths-inch rope which is easy to work with, yet strong enough to be dependable. Fasten a carabiner to the base of one of the stanchions where the bridle is attached. This prevents the rope from slipping up and possibly breaking the stanchion. It is important that the carabiner (or a small loop) goes *through* the bridle that is wrapped around the stanchion. This puts the pressure on the rope and not on the stanchion. Remember, the dogs are pulling at the other end of this bridle and the pressure on the stanchion is balanced out by the dogs.

A small loop can be substituted for the carabiner and attached to the stanchion where the bridle is wrapped around at the base of the runner. It must be SMALL, not longer than three inches, and not in a position where it can catch on anything on the trail. This could be very dangerous and could break a runner or stanchion or even hurt the dogs.

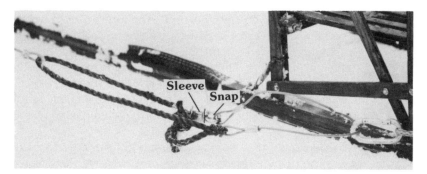

Here the quick-release snap is closed and locked. The snap is inside of the metal sleeve and closed. Pulling back this sleeve will release the little snap and free the cable.

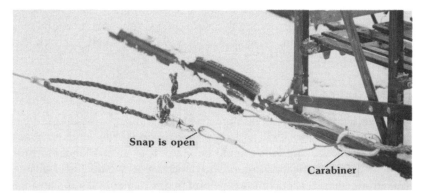

Here the quick-release snap is open, releasing the cable so it could slip through the caribiner (which has been run through the rope on the stanchion). This is where the bridle has been tied off.

Here the rope release is used. You can see how the loop is used, bringing the rope through the loop and placing a stick through it to hold the cart. This double-tubular nylon webbed material makes the kind of release that slips well, but you have to watch for wear.

Tie the snap on one end of a ten-foot rope. The rope needs to be this length so that you can tie it to a tree or stationary object and still have plenty of rope left to secure your sled or cart. Tie the rope around the base of a tree or to the bumper of your vehicle and bring the cart or sled over to it. Snap the quick-release snap into the carabiner (or loop) on the sled or to one of the upright stanchions on a cart in a place where you can reach it. Push the vehicle ahead to tighten the rope. Now you are ready to hook up the team.

You must take some precautions when using this snap. First, check your rope for wear or for knots. Make sure the snap works freely and closes securely. Once I had a snap accidently open as I was hooking up a six-dog team. My team is very strong and always anxious. I had just gone to get Zak and Nanook, the brawn of my team, when the snap came loose. All there was time to do was grab the brushbow as it went screaming by. Of course, it knocked my down and the team dragged me a quarter of a mile before I could stop them. Now, it is embedded in my mind to check that snap!

An Alternate Method

There is another way to fashion a make-shift quick-release, and I use this method most often. Take a piece of rope about ten feet long and make a loop at one end. The loop should be about four inches long. Run the end of the rope with the loop *around* the stanchion or *through* the carabiner. Taking the loop, place it *over* the rope and pull enough of the rope through the loop so that you can put a smooth stick, peg, or piece of tubing through it. Pull the rope tight until the peg fits tightly against the loop.

To release, just pull the peg out and the rope will slip off the sled or cart. This is fast and really easy to use. Just make sure you are near enough the post or object you've tied so you can reach the peg.

When training I use two posts for a tie-off area. I secure the tie-off rope to one of the posts; then I bring the cart or sled over, line it up, and tie off. After I have pushed the vehicle forward until the release rope is snug, I attach the gangline and straighten it out. Next, I bring the dogs to the hook-up station. I use a stake-out chain fastened between the posts with twelve-inch leads coming off the main chain. This keeps the dogs right next to me, the sled is close, and I can quickly hook up and be on my way.

8
Transporting and Restraining Your Team

The stake-out chain is a chain with leads off it needed to tie your team at a given place. The stake-out chain may be hooked between two trees, between two posts, between two vehicles (I have seen as many as fifteen dogs hooked up this way at a race), or along side of a vehicle. I have four two-foot pipes, one and a half inches in diameter, welded under the front and back bumpers on each side of my pickup truck. I insert a three-foot pipe into a larger pipe and run a bolt through holes drilled into both pipes. At the end of the three-foot extension I screw an eyelet bolt to which I hook my stake-out chain. This prevents the dogs from scratching my truck. Some drivers screw the eyelet bolts right onto the side of their truck and attach an eighteen-inch chain with a snap at each end to hold the dogs, but the dogs really do a job on the side of the truck when they get excited.

You can fasten these eyelet bolts onto the front and back bumpers, too, without having to weld pipes. However, by mounting pipes on the side, I can drive the truck foreward or move it without taking the chains off. Sometimes I will hook both pipes on one side and then put a four-dog gangline in between them as a way of training four dogs with the truck. I can train a four, six, or eight-dog team this way and control the speed. You have to be especially careful when you come upon another car when making this type of training run.

Stake-out chains are necessary at a race since there are so many dogs. If you use rope an excited dog could chew the line and set himself free. Be sure to use only the best chain—galvanized or coated—because a dog can get lead poisoning from an uncoated chain. The snaps should be of good quality brass. Plastic-coated aircraft cable is both strong and nice looking, and it doesn't rust like chain. While it is more expensive and takes more work, it makes a great line to work with. Eight dogs are maximum for aircraft cable line.

STAKE-OUT CHAIN

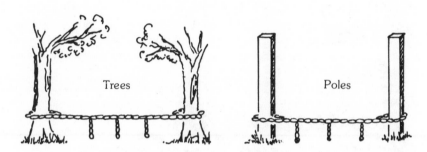

Trees

Poles

CHAIN

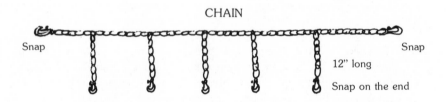

Snap

Snap

12" long

Snap on the end

AIRLINE CABLE

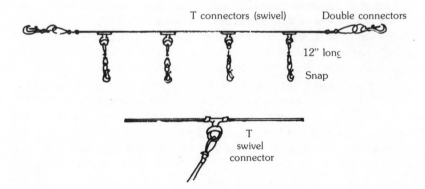

T connectors (swivel)

Double connectors

12" long

Snap

T
swivel
connector

HOW TO MAKE A CHAIN STAKE-OUT LINE

Measure the distance you need for the length of the chain. I would use the length of the truck, because it is the most useful place to hook a team. Next, you need to know how many dogs you plan to hook up. I hook six on each side of my truck. If you need eighteen feet of chain for the length of your truck and are running four or five dogs, add twelve- to fourteen-inches per dog for the leads coming off the main chain. Then you will need an "S" fastener to attach each lead to the chain, and another "S" fastener to attach each snap to the lead. This fastener is also used to attach a snap at either end of the main chain so it can be snapped into the eyelets.

It will depend on how many dogs you hook up as to how far apart the leads will be, but give each dog plenty of room and don't crowd them. They need at least three to four feet between the leads. Ed, a friend of mine, uses a twenty-five foot roll of chain with leaders every four feet. I have seen Ed hook onto his truck and then to a tree some fifteen feet away to give his dogs plenty of room.

Again, consider how many dogs you are going to be tying. With airline cable eight dogs maximum are recommended. A hardware store would be your best bet in getting this type of cable and all of the fittings you will need to put it together. Make sure you have swivel connectors and snaps with swivel ends so that the line does not tangle. A dog can choke himself to death if not on a swivel snap. *Crimp* each of the connectors carefully so that they don't come apart, as there will be a lot of tension on the line when you are hooking up your team. Like the chain stake-out line, you will need a snap at each end of this line to hook onto a tree or your vehicle.

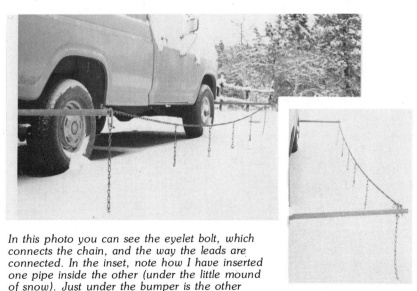

In this photo you can see the eyelet bolt, which connects the chain, and the way the leads are connected. In the inset, note how I have inserted one pipe inside the other (under the little mound of snow). Just under the bumper is the other eyelet holding the pipe in place.

The dogs on a stake-out line alongside of the truck. See how the chain is fastened to the eyelets at the end of the pipe. Make sure you use a swivel snap at each collar.

When I first started running dogs, I tied them in the back of my pickup camper.

DOG BOXES OR CARRIERS

It seems that sled dog drivers are never quite satisfied to run close to home; they are always looking for a special place where they can run their team and train without running into cars, motorcycles or cross-country skiers. So they hit the road with their teams loaded into dog boxes, the sled on top, and the truck filled with all the necessary junk they can't seem to run without. And they head for the high country.

The dog box is designed to hold from four to twenty dogs when a driver is transporting his team to a race or for training. Each box is designed to hold one dog comfortably and is usually filled with straw for warmth and to help the dog's damp coat after a run. Dogs perspire through their tongues, so their faces are usually covered when they come in from a run.

There are many styles of dog boxes. At the sprint races, you'll see every type of dog box imaginable, from trailers with a dog box attached to it, to ultra-fancy rigs. The drivers that are running the circuit have some incredibly fancy rigs. One was a molded fiberglass van with a camper place where people could relax and keep warm—as well as luxurious places for the dogs. Others look held together with bailing wire, with chewed wooden doors that sort of hold in the dogs. One night a driver I know had a dog *eat* his way out of his dog box. He had to get up at 3:30 a.m. to put him into another box. You could hear that dog chewing all night.

Not everybody has a dog box. When I first started, I used to tie my dogs in the back of my camper shell. No matter if you transport them in an open pickup, but be sure to TIE YOUR DOGS SO THEY DON'T FALL OUT.

Notice the chain hanging down below the door. When the doors are closed, I put this chain up and lock it into a keeper which is located at the bottom right side of the last door. It is always a good idea to be able to lock your dogs in the dog box. You wouldn't want to lose a dog. This is Nekko, my lead dog.

53

This dog carrier is attached to a flat-bed trailer. Sandy runs Malamutes and can carry eight in this trailer. He carries a long toboggan sled plus a race sled. Notice how long this sled is.

Val and Brenda carry as many as eighteen dogs in this box. They each run two or three teams at the races.

The size of the dog box you make will of course depend on how many dogs you intend to carry, but remember it's always nice to have extra room, because you may end up running more dogs as time goes on.

The dog box is usually built from half-inch and five-eighths inch plywood. The area for the dog should be large enough for him to lie down comfortably. There must be *good ventilation*. Cut 3x4 inch squares and put a heavy wire mesh on the inner wall of each stall so there is cross-ventilation through the entire box. The doors should have large holes that are covered with very heavy mesh so the dog can get plenty of air but not stick their heads out or by hit by rocks from on-coming cars. The box should be bolted onto the truck and "lock-washers" should be used with *two* nuts on each bolt. This will cause the nuts to inter-lock. On bumpy roads, these nuts can work loose and should be checked often.

Some drivers with only three dogs use airline carriers in the back of their station wagons or vehicles. It is also a good idea to have some place to put the dogs after a run, whether a race or training run. The dogs should be cooled down before putting them into the dog box or it will be like a "Sauna Box." I let mine cool for ten or fifteen minutes before I load them, and this gives me time to give them a drink of water and take their harness off. It you are running a hound or hound-mix, don't let the dogs get chilled before you load them, and use plenty of clean dry straw for them to snuggle into. This will be especially helpful if you have just run in a blizzard and the dogs are wet from the snow packing in their coats. Under these conditions I put the dogs away as soon as I can. They will need water, so be sure to carry their dog dishes and a container of water for them.

Here is another trailer, but look at how this driver has inserted the plastic airline carriers into specially designed holders. This way he can take the carriers out if needed.

This dog box has a tack room for all the harnesses and equipment. There are other styles of tack boxes, too.

When you unload a dog from your dog box, don't ever unload him like this! *Take the dog by the collar, put one arm under his stomach and gently lift him out. Dogs will probably try to jump out on their own, and that's all right, but make sure you have an arm under them so when they hit the ground you can slow them down. If a dog jumps from these heights, he can injure a shoulder or leg. Let him down gently, if you can. Sometimes when you open the box the dog becomes spring-loaded!*

Still another idea for a dog carrier. This driver can carry sixteen dogs.

9
Clothing

As with any winter sport, the clothing you need will, of course, depend on what part of the country you live in and how cold it gets. In the areas where the temperature drops below zero, your clothing will need to be much warmer, yet must breathe to allow perspiration and moisture from your body to escape.

Layering is recommended. To over-dress can be as dangerous as under-dressing. Layering allows unwanted clothing to be taken off when you get warm. Wool is one of the warmest materials to wear. The new line of polypropylene is very good, also. There are so many new materials and name-brand clothing on the market today, it would be very difficult to list them all.

You don't have to have fancy clothing, just warm comfortable, clothes that do the job. They will be dirty, torn and smelly by the time spring comes. I wear an army field jacket with a liner for general purposes and training. When the weather gets really cold I add a heavy goose-down parka.

Warm gloves are most important for your joy in running sled dogs. I haven't found a better glove than the *Patagonia* bunting liner for the inside of mittens or worn by itself. It is made of polypropylene bunting that looks like navy blue sweat-shirt material. The warmth is unbelievable. I use the liners with a pair of fur or *Gore-tex* mittens. Propylene socks are great too.

WIND CHILL CHART

WHAT THE THERMOMETER ACTUALLY READS (°F)

50	40	30	29	10	0	-10	-20

WIND SPEED   WHAT IT EQUALS IN ITS EFFECT ON EXPOSED FLESH

WIND SPEED	50	40	30	29	10	0	-10	-20
CALM	50	40	30	20	10	0	-10	-20
5	48	37	28	16	6	-5	-15	-26
10	40	28	16	4	-9	-21	-33	-46
15	36	22	9	-5	-18	-36	-45	-58
20	32	18	4	-10	-25	-39	-53	-67
25	30	16	0	-15	-29	-44	-59	-74
30	28	13	-2	-18	-33	-48	-63	-79
35	27	11	-4	-20	-35	-49	-64	-82
40	26	10	-6	-21	-37	-53	-69	-85

◀—— **LITTLE DANGER IF PROPERLY CLOTHED**

DANGER OF FREEZING EXPOSED FLESH

DANGER **GREAT DANGER**

There are two thicknesses, light-weight and heavy-weight. I use the heavy-weight because my feet get cold so easily.

Polypropylene material is made from a spun plastic and manufactured in such a way that the material actually *breathes*. It wisps away the moisture from perspiration and keeps the body dry. One would think because it is plastic it would do just the opposite, but it doesn't. Polypropylene is used to make jackets, gloves, face masks, socks, pants and long underwear. *North Face, Patagonia,* and *Moonstone* are three companies that use this material.

Thinsulate is another light-weight material used for lining sleeping bags, jackets, gloves and boots. It is warm and, being light-weight, is very desirable for clothing. This material is being used in mountaineering expeditions. *Thinsulate* material is manufactured by 3M Company of microscopic synthetic fibers that hold trapped air better than the same thickness of insulation.

JACKETS

Your jacket should be light-weight yet warm; a non-tear outer shell is recommended because when dogs jump on you their toenails often rip a jacket. The jacket should be somewhat water-proof, because melting snow will cause dampness, and it must be comfortable so you can move around without being restricted. Weight is a consideration because of the running you do with a team. If your jacket is heavy and cumbersome, you could become overheated, and the added weight will slow you down. As for the best color—*dark*! My pretty bright, red jacket is now a dark brownish red color from the dog hair, mud, dog food, and you name it. Layering with a long underwear top, a turtleneck T-shirt and a wool sweater will ensure that you stay warm. If the weather is very cold wear a bunting jacket and a parka and you'll be quite toasty.

GLOVES

My favorite subject, gloves, are one of the most important items of equipment. Hands can be frostbitten so easily in this sport, so they need special attention. I've tried all kinds of gloves over the years and, as most drivers will agree, I have to have a glove that can be easily removed when working with the snaps on the ganglines.

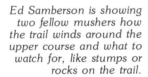

Ed Samberson is showing two fellow mushers how the trail winds around the upper course and what to watch for, like stumps or rocks on the trail.

59

The *Gore-tex* glove lined in *Thinsulate* is a great glove. You can also purchase this in a mitten that is waterproof as well as warm. But please, *don't* EVER USE A WOOL GLOVE OR MITTEN WHEN RUNNING YOUR TEAM! A wool glove or mitten is great when you are hooking up the dogs or just messing aroung, but you should NEVER wear them while running, because they will not keep out the cold air. The air will travel through the glove causing frostbite. If you run at 20 MPH and the temperature is zero degrees, the wind chill should be thirty-nine degrees below and your hands and flesh, if exposed, would freeze in just a few seconds. Thus, the importance of clothing that fits well and is warm!

FACE MASK

A balaclava or face mask is another important item. When the temperature starts to drop and the face is exposed, the skin takes a beating. A man's beard will pack with ice and sometimes a woman's face will also pack with ice if she has any facial hair.

The polypropylene face mask is best because it doesn't freeze from moisture around the mouth and nose. If you get too warm, lift it up and cool off. The balaclava is a hood that covers the whole head, leaving an opening for the eyes. The mouth is covered for added protection from cold in the lungs. There are also wool and acrylic face masks that have eye and mouth openings, but they have a tendency to freeze up and pack with ice. Tuck a balaclava inside of your jacket and in a few minutes, just from the heat of the body, it will be dry and ready to wear again.

SOCKS

There are many theories about how many pairs of socks to wear, which material is the warmest, and whether a liner should be worn with a heavier sock. See what works best for you as an individual. If you wear a good heavy polypropylene sock with boots that fit will, you shouldn't have cold feet. I tried all kind of socks, used two pairs, had the metallic liners with a wool sock over that and nothing worked until I found the Patagonia heavy duty socks. Try different brands and see what works best for you. Some people will use a silk liner with a wool sock over it. Silk liners are designed for skiers, who don't move their feet very much, but we run a lot while driving dogs and a liner can slip and bunch up. Whatever sock you choose, remember to change when they become damp, because this is how you get frostbite.

LONG UNDERWEAR

Here, again, are many types to choose from, and if you are one of those people who don't feel the cold as much as the rest of us, you may not even need heavy long underwear. "Longjohns" are now made of silk, polypropylene, cotton fiber mixed with silk, a "fish-net" type of material, and of course the old stand-by, red flannel. The union suit is one piece. I prefer a two piece set. It doesn't matter what brand you choose as long as they work well for you. Change every day as they collect moisture and become less effective if they are salty from perspiration.

BOOTS

Well-fitting rubber boots are recommended. They should have a thick felt liner for warmth. The *Sorel* is ideal for running dogs and comes in many styles. It is especially designed for cold weather and is waterproof. I wear the *Snow Cat*. It is designed for snowmobiling and is very warm. Be sure to take the socks you will be wearing when you go to purchase boots, so you can make sure of getting a good fit. I have worn the Alaskan Muk-luks, too. Sorel also makes a Muk-luk. However, they are leather and eventually, even though treated, will absorb moisture.

The army makes a boot called "The Mickey Mouse" boot for military use in Alaska. Many drivers use them on the distance runs because they are so warm. You'll find them at army surplus stores, with a great deal of wonderful other goodies we use in this sport, i.e., nylon webbing, snaps etc.

I knew I wore a padded hat for something. This is the easiest way to move a sled; they are so awkward to carry. This way you are less likely to hit someone.

HATS

A driver is known by his or her hat, which can become a sort of status symbol. Fur hats have become the rage in sledding because they are so warm. They have been used in the Northwest and in Alaska for years. However, any warm hat will do nicely. If you run dogs at night you might want to consider using a head-lamp and seeing how it will fit over your newly-acquired head piece. A simple wool ski hat is also quite effective.

As I mentioned before, you could spend a year's wages on clothing if you wanted to, but what really counts is comfort and warmth. When it gets really cold and windy, pull on some nylon wind-resistant pants with elastic at the ankles and the waist, or pull an old pair of sweat pants over your jeans. They really make a difference, especially at night when it feels so much colder.

Kent Allen, a director for the International Sled Dog Racing Association here in Colorado, has run dogs for a long time. He is always there to help when needed getting the dogs in and out of the starting gate.

10
The Team

There is a definite "musher's lingo," terminology used by drivers so their dogs all know the same commands.

Gee—right turn.

Haw—left turn.

Gee Over—to move to the right to pass another team or to run on the right side of a road or trail.

Haw Over—same as above, but to run on the left side.

Gee/Haw Come—to have your leader come to you and turn the team around. This is an asset in case you cannot leave the sled or cart. You may have made a wrong turn and need to turn the team around quickly or perhaps came to a dead-end in the trail.

Trail—to ask for "trail" in a race means you want to pass, and the driver ahead of you has to stop and hold his team until you have gone by.

On-by—to pass a turn-off or to keep the team going when you pass another driver. Sometimes the dogs want to stop and investigate something they shouldn't.

HIKE!—to start the team from a standing position.

Whoa!—the command to stop the team.

THE MAKING OF A TEAM

A team can consist of one dog, if that is all you have to run, or more commonly three or more dogs run on a gangline in an orderly manner. (Well, as orderly as any sled dog can run.) The first dog in the line-up is your lead dog. The dogs behind him are called the "point" or "swing" dogs. After these two dogs come the team dogs—the motor, if you will—of the team. They keep it going. The leader leads, the point or swing dog helps the leader bring the team around, and the team dogs move the sled ahead. Next in line are the wheel dogs. These guys have the awesome duty of turning the sled. They take all the shock from the gangline on starts and stops. They must be good strong dogs, not necessarily fast, but very even tempered as they motivate the team.

Running a double hitch, two abreast, is preferred. If you have an uneven number of dogs, put one in the middle by himself; run a double wheel and a double lead. Sometimes you will have a dog that likes to run lead alone, which can solve a multitude of problems.

Every dog in the team needs to learn to *pull* and know some of the commands, such as *Whoa*, *On-by*, and *Stand*. These are the basic commands you use so much it isn't hard for the dogs to pick them up.

If you can, move all of your dogs around to the different positions on a team. You will have only one lead dog, but you can put another dog up front with him. Some dogs run better on the left side and others run better on the right—be sure to pay close attention to this. A dog should track straight ahead. He should not run on top of the gangline, but slightly away from it, so that he is not likely to get tangled or step across it. One of the first steps in putting a team together is to decide which dogs are best suited for each position. There are some basic reasons for making these decisions.

THE LEAD DOG

A lead dog should know some commands, however his main function is to hold out the gangline and take the team down the road. Dogs that have been trained to take commands are worth a great deal of money and have sold for as much as $5000. It takes a great deal of time and energy to train a lead dog. Not very many drivers have a command-trained leader, except, of course the top drivers who are driving for a living, or people who will take the time to train a dog for that position or those who are driving large teams. Driving a large team without a command leader is like driving a semi-truck without a steering wheel.

The lead dog can be a mutt or a purebred. He has to have a special desire to please, take commands, and adjust to the stress of leading a team.

The lead dog has to have control over his team. The other dogs must respect and be willing to follow him, so choose a dog that is a little more

A 6:00 a.m. training run! This is what it looks like running seven dogs all lined out like they're supposed to be. It is a beautiful time to run and what a wonderful way to start a day!!

aggressive, not a fighter, that demands respect. A scrappy, aggressive dog does not belong anywhere on your team. The lead dog must drive hard the whole time he is in harness to keep his team lined out. He must want to lead and know he has earned the right to be there. Lead dogs take on an "attitude" when they are in the lead position. They will take commands willingly and keep the team out of trouble when passing another team. If the only commands he knows are *on-by* and *HIKE*, if your leader will at least pay attention when you are talking to him, he will get you down the right trail.

The lead dog must be bold enough to lead his team though situations that may frighten him at first glance, like a creek bed with water running through it or a cover of thin ice which he breaks through. He may have to lead his team over a cattle guard or through a gate, maybe over a bridge. If he goes over or through something the team knows it is alright to follow.

Having two leaders will help to off-set stress and help encourage confidence.

Dan MacEachen of Aspen, Colorado, takes tourists on guided trips through some of the most beautiful country. Here, Dan is driving his team of seventeen dogs, including Malamutes, Alaskan Huskies, and Siberian Huskies. As you can see, the sled dog is still being used for hauling and earning a living. Dan is one of only a handful of men doing this today. His dogs are well-behaved and well-trained. He has over 260 dogs in his kennel and is also helping to train Will Steger's team for the next Arctic trip.

If you would like information regarding this service of touring, contact Dan at Snowmass, Colorado.   (Photo courtesy of Dan MacEachen, Aspen, Colorado)

Bruce Harper's on his way at the Steamboat Springs, Colorado, race. His team are all AKC Siberian Huskies.

A six-dog hitch.

CHOOSING YOUR LEAD DOG

Most of the time your lead dog will be the dog you have spent the most time with, the dog you have owned and that listens to you. If you are going to buy a leader, remember that not all leaders will lead for everybody. What kind of leader do you need—a leader that will lead a three-dog team or one that that can lead twenty dogs down the trail? Does he have to know *all* of the commands or just hold out the line and be able to follow the scent of the previous team? It is an asset, too, to have a dog that can follow a trail. Remember, if there is a blizzard and you can't see, your lead dog must be able to follow the trail by scent.

Your lead dog does not need to be a large dog or run exceptionally fast, but he must be able to stay ahead of the team. He should be able to think for himself when you are not sure of the trail; there again the *nose* takes over.

If your leader is doing his job, leave him alone. He doesn't need you to carry on a conversation with him. You can, of course praise him once in a while.

He will be a sensitive dog, very eager to learn and to please you. If you train your own leader, and I strongly recommend that you do, make sure there is a certain trust between you. *Know* the dog before you start to train him.

POINT OR SWING DOGS

These dogs can be the second string leaders that can replace a tired or injured lead dog. They are sometimes command leaders, if you are fortunate enough to have this many. On large professional teams there will be as many as six command leaders on a five hundred mile race, and especially on the Iditarod.

Point dogs need to be fast enough to stay out in front and help the lead dog keep the team going; and if they are the *meat* of the team (if you are running six) they will need to be strong. As mentioned earlier, they should know the commands "On-by" and "Whoa" as well as "Hike!" They do pick these up when you are teaching them to pull.

On larger teams of eight or more, point dogs help the lead position by bringing the team around on corners and keeping the gangline stretched out. They are ususally your faster dogs and encourage the team with their enthusiasm.

THE TEAM DOGS

The meat of the team, the power, the brawn, the heart of your team are the team dogs. They love to pull and are always into their tuglines. Their tails should be down when they are pulling, for if a tail goes up while they are running they aren't doing their job. If you have fast leaders, you'll need fast team dogs. These dogs are just "the good ole boys"—they go down the road and pull straight ahead. A lot of good team dogs have come right from the county pound. Look at it this way, you are giving them a good home and not asking too much from them—just a little run down a snow covered trail. A friend of mine did this and called his team "the pound hounds."

THE WHEELERS

The wheel dogs are the strongest, and are usually the slowest, dogs. My wheel dogs, Zak and Nanook, are the team's motivation. Nanook will let the dogs rest only a few seconds before he starts yapping to get the team moving again. Wheel dogs must be taught to pull, to use their strength to keep you out of the treeline, and corner the sled.

When you are driving a sled or cart you must be careful not to run over your wheel dog—they can be hurt so easily. The gangline has to be watched at all times to make sure there isn't any slack in it. If there is and the sled takes up that slack, it is the wheel dogs that get the *snap* from the gangline. They take all the shock from the sled from the first "Hike" to the last "Whoa" of the run, so be sure to take care of them. Watch that you don't slam the sled or cart into their legs. These dogs are followers and seldom make good leaders. They will usually keep looking back to see what is following them. This puts undo stress on them. However, you may need to put one in the lead in an emergency, so you should try them at some point in time.

Here again, watch to see which side of the gangline each dog runs best on. If a dog runs into the gangline, try him on the other side. He may not run well there either and may always be a dog that runs close to the center line.

If you are running only a three-dog team, I would advise a double wheel and a single lead. This will control the sled better. If you are running a team of hound-type dogs, keep a shorter distance between the hitches as hounds are used to running in packs and are chasers. If you are running a team of Nordic dogs use a greater distance between each set as they like room to run.

A Border Collie leads a team of Siberians and mixed breeds.

(Photo Courtesy of Janet Larson)

11
Training

Remember your dog is as new at this as you are, so go easy. You never want to fighten him with any of the equipment you are going to use. He has no idea what in the world you are doing to him and has probably never pulled anything thus far.

BASIC TRAINING EQUIPMENT

You will need some basic training equipment to get started with this first segment.

1. A collar with a strong ring on it.
2. A well-fitted harness.
3. A long lead rope (can be a piece of cotton rope, poly-rope or flat nylon webbed material).
4. A piece of polyethlene rope (water-ski rope), ten feet long.
5. A black bungie cord with hooks at each end.
6. One 'O' ring of brass or welded steel, two inches in diameter.
7. Two brass snaps (medium size).
8. A small log weighing about ten pounds (you can use 2x4's).

After you have gathered all of this wonderful equipment on your kitchen table, begin to put it together. First take your lead rope and put a snap at one end of it and tie a loop for your hand at the other end. Now take the ten foot poly-rope and put the ring at one end and the snap at the other. Here's how you do it. When you push this type of rope together it will open up and you can insert the rope into itself. Put the ring on one end, form a loop with the ring in it and push the rope together about seven inches from the end, insert the end through the opening in the center of the rope so that you have a small loop with the ring in it. Pull the rope tight. The outside rope will tighten around the inside rope and won't come out.

Take the black bungie cord and insert the "S"-hooks into the poly-rope. Now stand on the poly-rope and pull the bungie cord and the rope. Stretch the bungie and fasten it to the poly-rope and clamp the "S"-hooks closed. This will provide ample *give* when the rope is stretched; the bungie works as a shock absorber. Put this bungie cord about two feet from the "O" ring. Using the same technique as you used to put the ring on, attach a snap to the opposite end of the rope, and you have a modified training gangline.

Now you are ready to harness up your dog. Make sure the collar is over the harness. Snap the lead rope you made onto the collar. Think about the area in which you'll be training. It can be down the sidewalk or a dirt road, but make sure it is free of obstacles and relatively free of activity and fairly flat in the beginning. Do you have a tree or post to tie the dog where you will be training him?

Lead the dog to the tie-off area and tie him up while you get the log and the other line with the bungie cord in it. This will make the dog understand that he is to be tied before a run.

Bring the log and rope over to where the dog is and attach the rope to the log by wrapping it around the log twice and running the rope through the O-ring. This should hold securely. Straighten out the rope with the snap at the end. Now bring Fido over to where the snap is lying. He'll probably sit down. Make him get up and face *away* from the gangline in the direction you want him to travel. Fasten the snap into the small loop at the end of the harness. Now you must realize, he isn't going to know what has attached itself to him and he will do one of two things, either sit down and say, "Forget you," or he could walk on as if nothing at all has taken place. Most of the time a dog will balk because of the noise coming from the logs dragging on the dirt. Take hold of the lead line that is attached to his collar and gently persuade him to come. He'll run sideways, turn around and try to go back and sniff at this "thing that's chasing him." Say, "NO" and coax him forward. Make him understand that this is work, NOT play time. Keep your voice happy and give him lots of praise and love when he moves out. After a few feet, stop him by saying "Whoa." Pet him and tell him what a good boy he is, then start walking again, giving the command "Hike." This is the command to go. Keep the lessons short—ten or twelve minutes. After that he becomes bored.

By the end of the first session your dog should be pulling the log fairly well. He'll probably trot a little sideways at first, but that's okay. Make sure the harness isn't binding him anywhere nor too tight around his neck.

Repeat this same procedure for three or four days until your dog will pull the log without paying attention to it. Then gradually increase the weight to about twenty-five pounds.

STEP TWO

The next step is teaching him to stand still while he's being hooked up. If your dog already knows the commands "Sit," "Stay," and "Down," you're ahead of the game. If he doesn't, you have to teach him at least the stay.

By taking one or two logs and wrapping the poly-rope around them and pulling it through the "O" ring, you have a perfect pull-toy for the dog's first lesson.

When the dog first starts out he may run like this.

Nekko, our lead dog, has to start out the same as any other sled dog. As you can see, he's pulling to one side and about to run over the trainer. The hard part is keeping the dog from getting in your way and tripping you.

This time tie off the logs to something stationary, a tree, a post or even the front of your car. (If he's a big dog you might want to make sure your brake is on!) Bring the dog to the log and snap the gangline to his harness. Pull the dog *forward* just a little to tighten the line. Take the lead you have in your hand and drop it onto the ground; put your foot on it to hold him still. The dog must look straight ahead and hold the line out taut. If he moves or tries to sit down tell him "NO" and make him stand. This can become very boring to the dog after he has been used to going on as soon as he is hooked up. Practice this until the dog will stay long enough for you to go to the tie-off and unhook it. Be sure to have the lead in your hand before you unhook him. The quick-release will work well here. When you finally get to the point when you release the tie-off (without him coming back and helping you), yell out "Hike" and stand aside, because he will probably take off like a shot.

At this point you start to drop back from the dog's side. Work him until you can run behind him at the end of the lead rope. If he stops to water a tree or smell the flowers, say "On-by," "On-by," and make him go on. You don't want him to get into the habit of stopping when ever he wants to. *YOU MUST ALWAYS BE IN CONTROL*. Be sure to praise him when he goes by something you know he wants to stop and smell. Can you imagine what would happen if a dog in a twelve dog hitch stopped to smell something? He would be dragged and possibly injured. *He must be obedient*.

At this point you have already figured out that *you* are more tired than Fido when the session is over. Right? Be sure *you* warm up a little, too, before you start to train because, believe me, this is only the beginning. A dog recuperates four time faster than a human, so when you are just getting your second wind, he is ready to go again.

Repeat each lesson for a few days until the dog knows what is expected of him. It helps when you are hooking up a whole team to teach them to *sit* while you hook up. This gives you even more control over the situation, as the dogs can get terribly excited.

When you can run at the full length of the rope and the dog will listen and obey your commands, will stay when you hook him up, and can easily pull around twenty-five pounds, he is ready for bigger and better things.

At this point he has learned to pull and knows three commands: "Whoa," "On-by," and "Hike." It is important that he consistently obeys these commands. The "On-by" command is especially important. It is used for all kinds of situations on the trail. For instance when the trail forks to one side or the other and you want your team to go straight, you will use "On-by." When passing another team and you must keep going, use "On-by." This is especially helpful when you come upon a loose dog. Your team must learn to go by these distractions at your command. Again, *you should always be in control of the dog*. Know what you want your dog to do *before* you get into a confusing situation. Never loose your temper. A dog only does what he knows to do and it is up to you to make sure he clearly understands what is expected. It is so important to have a good communication with the dog you are working with. Make sure he has learned each step before going onto the next one. Then refresh him often by reviewing what he has learned.

By the second or third lesson the dog should be pulling straight down the road and leaning into his harness. See how this veteran sled dog is pulling into her harness.

The trainer is teaching Nekko to hold the line out and stand still while the rest of the dogs are being hooked into the gangline. A hand on the dog's neck to reassure him that this is where you want him to stay seems to help.

If you are starting a young puppy, begin slowly and with minimal weight. This three-month-old pup is pulling a four-foot 2x4. She grew up pulling and will be a good sled dog. As you can see, she's moving right along.

YOUR FIRST RIDE

Now, let's go for a ride! Get your bicycle out and oil it up. (If you don't have one you can usually pick one up at a flea market nearby.) Attach the gangline to the bicycle and tie the bicycle to something stationary. Then go and get your sled dog. Snap him onto the gangline, pull the quick-release, and go for a spin. Make sure you do this little exercise where you can't get hurt—a park or a lonely dirt road is good. It should be free of obstacles and the quieter the better. Your dog will listen better and there will be less chance of a dog running out to interrupt the run.

The first run like this shouldn't be too long; a dog has to build his strength and endurance before he can run for long distances. A half a mile is a good start. Stop often and rest, making sure your dog keeps the line out and doesn't turn around and come back to you. That's a no-no.

As the days go by and you and your dog builds endurance, you can run him for two or three miles. Always check his feet when you get back, because running on gravel or hard ground will wear his pads. If his pads do get sore, put some salve on the foot and then put a bootie on him (a baby's sock will do nicely). Let him rest a couple of days before you run him again.

If you are only going to train one, two or three, I would train them this same way, one at a time. After you have trained two or three dogs and hooked them into a real gangline, the others are easy because you can just hook them up with the team that has already been trained and let them learn from the other dogs.

When you first start to hook your team to a cart, make sure the cart is tied off, then hook one dog in the gangline and make him stand there quietly until the entire team is hooked up.

A well-trained team should stand still on command. Here the ganglines are tight and the dogs are ready to go, yet they are awaiting my command.

As soon as they are lined out, turn 'em loose and let 'em run!

75

I will usually start my pups out in the training program I have just discussed. Then, when I feel they know what is expected of them, I put them into a team of veteran dogs. I do not want anything to go wrong when I first start them because they can become confused or frightened and refuse to run.

Let's say you have three dogs trained to pull your bicycle and you are looking into buying a cart and possibly a sled. (Outfitters that carry carts and sleds are listed in the Appendix.) By now you should have ordered a gangline, or made one.

When driving a cart or sled it is of the utmost importance to have a quick release system to hold your team.

The rope with a peg in it is great, cheap, and pretty fault-free. I use it a lot, and always find something to use for a peg if I need to. I usually attach the peg to the cart or sled with a piece of thin nylon string. I put a hole at one end and tie it on, because that way, when I pull free, the peg is still with me. You can also tie the rope you will be releasing from to the cart and just put it around the tree or post so the whole thing comes with you in case you have to tie off somewhere down the road.

To hook up, have your cart secured by the quick-release and the gangline attached to the front of the cart as illustrated in chapter 4. Bring the dogs over, one at a time, and tie them close to the cart. This is a good place to incorporate the stake-out chain. You can tie it off to two poles or trees and have the dogs right next to you where you will be hitching them.

Bring a dog over and fasten him to the gangline. Some drivers hook up the wheelers first and then work their way to the front of the team; others hook up the leaders first, and still others just hook up their calmest dogs first. If you train your dogs to be reasonably still, it won't matter too much which way you hook up. If you have a chewer, hook him up last, unless you have someone to watch him or her while you hook up the rest of the team. If he chews the gangline in two you'll find yourself chasing after the front runners of your team.

When you hook into the gangline, make sure that the neckline and tugline don't stretch the dog out like a banana. The dog should fit comfortably between these two lines. If the dog is long-bodied and the lines droop some, no problem. The dog will pull into the tuglines. Hook up the necklines first, then the tugs.

TANGLES

These unforeseen culprits can ruin a good run and seem to happen at the most inconvenient times, like at the starting chute or just as you approach a group of fans waving you on. A tangle can happen at any time when one dog crosses over another dog's line or steps over his neckline. The object in tow must be stopped, the brakes put on or a snow hook set, and the dog has to be undone. If he runs very far, he could be cut by the rope or dragged if the team goes down a hill. Some tangles can be so frustrating that you may have to unhook the whole team to straighten them out and just hope you can get them going before they get tangled up again.

A dog that is accustomed to running can sometimes get himself out of tangles. This is one more reason I believe in chaining dogs rather than putting them in a fenced area. On a chain they can learn to step out of this kind of situation. If one dog is tangled and not pulling straight, it will put a strain on the rest of the team. There have been nights when friends and I were running and would get a tangle that seemed to take forever. We ususaly ran eight to twelve dogs so you can imagine how many dogs we would have to separate. His team would come over to see mine as he was passing and cross over my team's ganglines. Or mine would come upon his team when in a tangle and want to get aquainted. Before we knew it, we had a jolly mess.

When hooking up your team, watch out for a dog that chews. Notice how Judi (pronounced Jedi) has the gangline in his mouth. This could be very costly since he can chew a gangline in half in less than 10 seconds, and the front of your team can be off and running. This is a "no-no."

"Up and over, Chinook, one more time!" Now if they will just stay untangled until I can release the team again.

12
Lead Dog Training

TRAINING THE TEAM'S "STEERING WHEEL"

Now that you have a little team together you'd probably like them to go where *you* want to go, instead of where *they* want to go. By now you should have one dog that has taken the initiative in taking your team down the road. You have already taught him to go *On-by*, *Whoa* and *Let's go* or *Hike*. If you have worked with this dog and he can sit, stay and maybe lie down, you are ready to start teaching him the attributes of a lead dog.

You will need an area free of noise, obstacles, cars and people—a place where it is quiet and the dog won't be distracted, and where you can make a short trail with loops that connect. This trail doesn't have to be over a quarter of a mile in length. Make the trail with a lawn mower or a hoe or simply use a trail that is already there. It will need some forks in it, one to the left and another to the right, or a straight trail with another trail splitting off.

Now that your dogs are in condition, running on foot will be a little more difficult than it was initially. So bring back the logs and have him pull these around while you run on foot behind him. A long leash on him will help. Use the long lead rope you trained with in the beginning.

78

MAKING THE TRAIL

When you have found a nice field to train in, take a hoe or rake and make a definite trail that the dog can easily see and follow. When you make a trail splitting off the main trail, make a loop and return to the original trail. Be sure this is wide enough and clear enough that the dog knows that there is a decision to be made here. This new trail should have a loop at the end so you won't have to stop and turn the dog around. Make some leads off to the right and some to the left, always wide enough so that no matter which way you are coming you can take either trail you choose. This way the dog must learn the *On-by* command. (See diagrams.)

Training trail:

All trails come into the main trail at one point or another.

Make the trail interesting

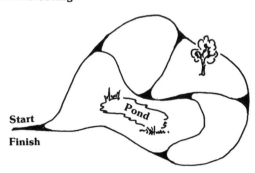

TAKING THE DOG THROUGH HIS PACES

Harness your new leader-to-be and if he's not too strong for you to handle on foot lead him across the course a few times. As you approach the trail you want, *before* you come to the intersection, give the command for that turn and pull him around. Tell him "Good-boy" and praise him. At this point you are just walking the dog over the course, getting him used to it. He may have a little trouble walking when he is used to running, but it is just another way of exercising control over your leader. After you have walked him over the whole trail for three or four days and he thinks he *knows* the trail, try to trot him over it. Remember, you must know which way you want to go before you get there (you can't expect the dog to learn commands if you don't know them). When you get to the turn-off tell him, "Gee, turn, Gee, Gee." If he makes a right turn, really get down and praise him. Make a big deal out of it. Then line him out again, making sure he is keeping the line tight. He must learn to stand still and wait for the command to go. Continue down the trail. When you come back to the main trail you will have another decision to make. Again, turn, stop and praise him for making the correct turn. (You must do this training every day or every other day for about three months before you can depend on him to take command in a stressful situation.)

After you have him taking commands while you run along side, start easing back so that eventually you are about ten feet behind. When you are sure he will listen to you, hook him up to the bicycle and practice this way. If he listens to you, hook up one more dog *behind* him and run two dogs. Remember, a dog has to learn through repetition, which takes a great deal of time and patience. After three or four months you'll see why lead dogs are so expensive, and may be willing to pay for one.

The dog must learn to obey you; you can not let him get away with running by a direct command to turn. That is a NO-NO! Stop him and *make* him go the way you commanded him to go. Don't let him get into bad habits! Line him out until the line is taut and start over. He must know this is not a play time but a time to learn. Don't work the dog over ten to fifteen minutes. If he's bored, he won't listen to you. I think the hardest part is containing the dog long enough to teach him something. He wants to run and doesn't particularly care where—"just let me run!" So you'll have to get his attention and tire him with the logs so you can work with him. I am a small person so my dogs can drag me all over the course before I can get them stopped unless I tire them out first.

You can use your own imagination. I'm sure that by now you have thought of all kinds of ways to train "Gee" or "Haw." A friend of mine used to bring his dog in the house and every time he got up the dog would follow, so he started giving commands. If he went to the kitchen and had a left turn to make he said "Haw." This worked so well he could take his team anywhere with this dog in the lead. I also knew a man whose team could

These two dogs, Nekko and Kishia, are my leaders so they are hooked together by a poly-rope with a snap at each end.

These leaders are more than just a little anxious. You will see a lot of dogs yelping and jumping in their harnesses wanting to go. You can't force a dog to run, they have to like it.

write his name in an open field, controlled only by voice command—NOW THAT'S IMPRESSIVE!

All this takes a great deal of patience and time, and the dog has to be a willing learner. Once you have one trained lead dog, you can hook the next lead-dog-to-be beside him and let the older dog train the new one. After a few dogs are trained, sledding becomes much easier. Just hook the new dogs up with the veterans and they do the training.

Now that your lead dog is trained and you have driven your team with the bicycle or cart, let's hook the team up to the sled. Make sure you have the sled secured to something solid. Hook the gangline to the sled's bridle. Straighten it all out—make sure the tugs are lined out and the necklines are where they belong. Check the snaps to see if any are in bad conditon and need to be replaced or have dirt cleaned out.

If you have made a stake-out line, have it handy so you can tie up the dogs. They are all harnessed, barking and yelping and ready to go.

Check your gear. Make sure you have your snow hook and an extra neckline or tugline. With the sled secure, the quick- release set, the gangline straight, bring your first dog, the one that will stand still while you hook up the others. If one dog is a chewer, hook him up last. One by one the dogs are all hooked into the gangline. Pull the quick-release and you are off!

As you glide through the snow covered country-side you will know that all the training, tangles, bruises and sore muscles were worth the effort. It is the most fantastic feeling in the world when the air is crisp and the dogs are running well!

Can you imagine riding through the forest on a sled like this in the quietness of winter with only the swishing of runners on the frozen snow? This is the Maroon Bells area near Aspen, Colorado.

Dan is driving a team of eleven dogs, with his passenger in the freight sled, touring Colorado's most famous sights. (Photo courtesy of Dan MacEachen, Aspen, Colorado)

13
Riding The Sled

Learning to ride a sled is like anything else, it takes time and practice, good balance, timing, and strength. If the sled runners are plastic, a sled will side-slip around turns, giving you the feeling it is going to go out from under you before you finish the turn. If the runners are exceptionally slick, they may side-slip even when you are going down a straight trail. You will soon become accustomed to this feeling and learn to use the side-slip to maneuver the sled around corners.

If possible, have someone with you the first time you take the sled out; it will help to give you more confidence. The sled feels much different than the cart and you have less control.

A good driver will help his team. When going up a hill the driver will hold on to the handlebow and run behind the sled, or will stand with one foot on the runner and *peddle* with the other foot, just like peddling a scooter. Bend down with the leg your weight is on and with the other foot push the sled forward with a long, sweeping stroke. It is a very graceful action. Watch the gangline and prevent it from going slack when you drive the sled forward with your foot—there is more to it than just giving the sled a push. If the gangline goes slack it will jerk the dogs needlessly and they will break their stride. So it has to be a smooth action, pushing, letting the sled slip, catching up to the dogs and again the push. Slowly counting

1 . . 2 . . 3 . . , 1 . . 2 . . 3 . . like a dance step, will help you get into the rhythm.

It takes a great deal of time and practice to master the peddling action. One way to practice, if you have someone to help you, is to hook a long rope onto the sled and have someone pull you in a vehicle. Be sure to have the driver go slowly, no more than 15 MPH, until you learn how to handle the sled. Go around some turns and practice this way.

This is fun and you can't really get hurt. You can't *lose* your team this way either! Get the *feel* of the sled *before* you hook your dogs to it. You can usually find a snow-packed road that is relatively free from traffic for practice.

To corner or turn to the left, stand on the left runner with your left foot placing your right foot behind the foot pad on the right runner and pushing out. This will spread the runners slightly, putting the weight on the left runner. At the same time pull up on the handlebow, lifting the front of the sled slightly off the snow, twisting it around the corner. It sounds difficult, but it really isn't, it just takes practice. And the faster you are going to go (to a point), the easier it is to corner. This is something you can learn while being pulled with a vehicle. To turn to the right, just reverse this procedure standing on the right runner and pushing out with the left foot.

Let's imagine that you're going down a long stretch of trail and you know a right turn is ahead and it is a pretty sharp corner. Try to steer the sled to the center of the trail by pushing out on one runner and slightly twisting the handlebow to make the sled move in that direction. As you approach this turn, let the dogs pull you around while you push *hard* on that runner. If it is a tight corner, bend down low for a good center of gravity and pull up on the handlebow, raising the front of the sled. It will slip right around the corner. Most people seem to find one turn easier than the other. I turn better to the left than I do to the right. I don't know why I feel awkward when I make a right turn but I have more trouble getting down and leaning into the corner. With practice you will get the hang of it.

When someone asks , "Do you just sit in the basket and let the dogs pull you?" show them this picture.

84

Now for the "killer hills." When you go down a hill, whether steep or gradual, NEVER LET YOUR BRUSHBOW HIT THE WHEEL DOGS. To slow the sled, you can use the sled's brake or you you can put your foot against the back stanchion, brace it, and dig your heel into the snow against the runner. You won't lose your balance because both feet are on the sled and you have weight on both of them. We use this technique a lot to slow the team down so they don't hear the brake. When dogs hear the brake they will *really* slow down and you may not always want to slow that much depending on the situation.

One thing to remember—a loose sled will NEVER tip over. I've seen mine, after being dumped, pop back up and go merrily down the road without me. Keeping a low center of gravity when cornering or going down a steep hill and braking helps prevent tipping.

When going uphill, peddle the sled. As you reach the top, stand on the runners and let the dogs pull you along. There may be times in cornering when you will have to literally get off the sled, run along the outside and pull the sled around a tight corner by the handlebow.

If you dump the sled, *REALLY TRY TO HANG ONTO THE SLED, DON'T LET GO UNLESS YOU RISK GETTING HURT!* Because if you lose the team you will have to chase them. The team should learn that if you dump the sled they should stop. Sometimes you will literally be whipped

Number 12 racing for the finish line with his team of Alaskan Huskies.

This is the Frank Hall "swivel sled." Notice that by twisting the handlebow to one side the runner is set at an edge.

off the sled by fresh or deep snow and you just can't hang on. But most of the time you can hang on and stop the team. A loose team can get hurt or hurt another team, so try to be careful and keep them under control.

To stop the sled, use the brake (in the middle of the sled under the basket) which should be easy for you to reach with one foot or the other. This will slow or stop a team but will not *hold* a team. You must set a snow hook to hold a team for any length of time. Slow the team until it stops, having the hook in your hand as you stand on the sled's brake. Set the hook either between the runners or just to the outside of the runner. Quickly press the hook deep into the snow with your foot. Then urge the team ahead slightly to *SET* the hook. *DON'T ever leave your sled without setting the hook.* You'll be chasing your team again.

Back to ganglines—if a gangline goes slack while you are going around a turn, the sled will drift outward then snap back as the dogs take up the slack. This can, and probably will, dump you so watch the slack. It can also hurt the dogs, especially the wheel dogs.

Dog sledding requires common sense and a lot of hard work. If you think things out and are prepared for the usual, you'll do fine. If you think *that* will never happen it probably *will*. Dogs can do some of the darnest things and really cause you to wonder if they *really are man's best friend*.

But, after you've traveled hundreds or even thousands of miles with them, you will have enormous love and respect for the dogs you have so painstakenly trained and guided over the snow-packed trails. It is a special sport, not for everybody, but for those who get hooked on it, there is nothing like it.

This driver is yelling for his team to give him all they have—a good fast start. Notice the plastic brushbow and handlebow. The handlebow is wrapped with twine.

14
Racing

Racing sled dogs has become one of the fastest growing winter sports in the world with the exception of skiing. Races are being held world wide, and the International Sled Dog Racing Association (ISDRA) is working on an organization that would govern races throughout the world.

Races are usually held from mid-December to late March. In order to have a sanctioned race, approved by ISDRA, certain rules must be followed. The trails have to meet special qualifications; a race has to have a certain number of timers, race marshals and stewards. This helps insure the best possible race conditions for a driver and his team. A tremendous effort goes into planning a race. The area must be chosen, the trail made and maintained every day to keep it open and hard packed. A committee has to be formed to mail the entry forms, receive them, and keep the record straight for ISDRA. Sponsors must be found to help offset expenses.

Finally starting time for the first race of the year is here. The chutes have been set up and groomed, the "Start" and "Finish" flags are hung over the proper chute, snow fence lines, the starting line and the finishing area. The little green "privys" are set here and there along the route.

Then the drivers start to come, one after another, filling the entire parking lot. Hundreds of dogs, all barking and yelping at once, are unloaded. To an outsider this must be a strange lot, people wearing everything from fur hats to tennis shoes. But they have one thing in common—they all LOVE their dogs and the sport that keeps them coming in the frigid winter weather. Something in this sport keeps them coming back. There are thousands of drivers racing dogs today and they will all tell you the same thing, "I don't know, I just love to do it."

HOW RACES ARE STARTED

The dogs are started in one or two-minute intervals. One team at a time will enter the starting chute. There the timer and starter will stand. A race marshal is usually present, too, along with handlers that help hold the sleds so the driver can go forward and see his team and get ready for the countdown. A 15-second countdown is called. The driver checks his sled, snow hook, dog-bag, and miscellaneous equipment. The 10-second time is called out; then five . . . four . . . three . . . two . . . one, and the team is off and running. The time is calculated from the time they leave until they return. A driver runs against the clock, not dog against dog. He has two chances to win, because most races are two-day events and times are added together. Some teams win by a mere 1/100 of a second.

TRAIL MARKERS

If the race is an ISDRA race, there will be markers for the mileage, and caution markers for any hazzard on the trail. There is also a sign that says, FREE ZONE. This sign means that the last one-half mile to the finish line a driver can pass at any time. The driver wanting to pass simply passes if he can and as fast as he can make his dogs go. Snow fences mark where another trail enters the main trail, or a caution area. There will be a marker for the three-dog class, the six-dog class, and the trail marker for the eight-dog class. The signs will usually be of a different color.

TRAIL ETIQUETTE

Trail etiquette is essential for the safety of the dogs and drivers. This sport is fun and everyone should have a good time and enjoy a safe run. There are always beginners just starting out, and they should be treated as professionally as the veteran drivers. When a driver gets so serious about winning that he forgets his manners, he no longer belongs on the trail.

When one driver comes up behind another driver it is customary to call out "Trail." The driver ahead should stop and let the faster team go by. He is to hold his team for one minute or until the other team is safely away. A passing driver has the right of way. He can ask the slower driver to halt his team or just slow down until he passes. If a driver has a problem on the trail, he should in no way block up the trail for the other drivers,

This is Kate and Dan Larkins' rig. Dan is a Gold Medal winner and he can carry sixteen dogs in this rig because he doubles them up. He wouldn't travel very far this way as the dogs get too cramped when they are doubled. He runs hounds and hound-mixes so they are a little smaller when they are curled up than the nordic dogs.

A last minute check-up before take-off. It pays to make sure everything is in its place and easily reached if needed. Pat's putting on the gangline getting ready to run.

however, sometimes this can't be helped and consideration and patience is a rule.

I've never seen a driver who wouldn't help another driver if he or she was in trouble. Races have even been lost because a driver stopped to help a new driver in trouble—and that's the way it should be.

A driver who comes upon a loose team should stop his team, put down his snow hook and, if possible, catch and tie-off the other team. Some day the loose team could be yours.

The starting chute of a sled dog race. The blackboard is used to write down the drivers' time. The long snow fence is to keep the team going straight down the trail.

When I hook up my dogs, I hook up the quiet ones first. The ones that will stand in place and hold out the gang-line. I have trained my leaders to hold the line out and stay put. I can use either of these dogs as leaders.

Always hook the neckline on first in case the harness slips out of your hand while hooking up the tugline.

TANGLES

A tangle is self-explanatory—the dogs cross over their lines, causing a tangle. Tangles have lost races for some of the best drivers. Sometimes you will have to undo almost the whole team before you can get straightened and going again. This is one hassel every driver would like to avoid. It can eat up seconds, even minutes, getting the dogs apart and a dog fight or even a breeding (if there is a bitch in season) can take place in the process.

SPRINT RACES

Sprint races, run at a distance of between three and ten miles, are the most commonly held local races.

Some teams are so fast and closely matched that they finish in less than tenths of a second of each other. Sometimes in the three-dog class the first teams will be coming in while the last of the three-dog class is still going out. This can happen in the six-dog class, too, if it is large enough.

"Come on Zak, be still a minute, or we'll never get this show on the road."

Then there's Judi, he is pure muscle and hard to harness. After you have trained your dog to GO! it can be hard to get him to STOP! They love to run and when you drag out the harnesses they go crazy.

91

To give you some idea of how fast an average team is run over a given course, I have outlined the *average and the top winning speed*.

3-Dog Class
Distance: 3 to 4 miles
Average speed: 15 to 18 MPH
Top speed teams winning the circuit run: 3 Mi. in 11.60 Min/Sec

6-Dog Class
Distance: 6 to 8 miles
Average speed: 15 to 22 MPH
Top speed teams winning the circuit run: 6 Mi. in 22.93 Min/Sec

8-Dog Class
Distance: 8 to 10 miles
Average speed: 18 to 28 MPH
Top speed teams winning the circuit run: 10 Mi. in 30.36 Min/Sec

Speed will increase with the number of dogs, not because the eight dog team dogs are faster, but because there are more dogs pulling and less weight resistance on any one dog.

MIDDLE DISTANCE RACING

Middle distance races are usually 25 to 150 miles long. Teams of six to fourteen dogs are run, depending upon the class. These dogs are trained

Here a driver gets help from another driver in the starting chute. The sled is held at the starting line and the countdown begins!

A good take-off. All the dogs are pulling and raring to go.

A team of Alaskans coming in at the Steamboat Springs race. It was 55 degrees on this particular day—too hot to run a race. The second day's race was run very early in the morning.

a little differently and will usually pace themselves to average 8 to 12 MPH over the entire course. However, there are the middle distance sprint races where the dogs are required to run at full speed (in a loop) at 22 MPH for thirty miles to the check stations. There they rest a few minutes and take off at that speed again. The John Beargrease is such a race. This race is 350 miles long and has a terrain like a roller coaster. Susan Butcher started the 1986 race with 18 dogs and finished with only five of her team. This is a very difficult race. One driver was overheard saying, "If I could train my dogs to run full speed for 200 yards, then trot for 200 yards, I'd have this race won."

Sometimes in the middle distance races, the driver must carry survival equipment on the sled which can weight fifty pounds. This race is usually a non-stop race against the clock, as are the sprint races. There is one exception, however—check-in stations are set up every twenty-five or thirty miles in the longer races. Sometimes the middle distance races are set up so the teams run twenty-five to thirty miles per day for two to three days, such as in the Glacier View and the Seeley Lake races.

LONG DISTANCE RACES

Long distance is entirely different than sprint racing. A team starts from point A and goes to point Z. There are mandatory stops and layovers with food drops for men and dogs. The teams will pace themselves at about 8 to 12 MPH and go for days, with the dogs covering an average of 100 miles per day at a trot. The Kuskokwin Race in Bethel, Alaska, is a 300-mile race run straight through with food drops and check-in stations every fifty miles where dogs and drivers are checked by a veterinarian and a physician. All dogs have to be examined at these points. If they are not fit to go on, they must be dropped from the race.

Here in the "lower 48", the Governor's Cup 500 mile race in Helena, Montana, is set up in the same way. It has an eight-hour mandatory layover and has check-in points, where the dogs are checked and the driver can get food for his dogs as well as rest if he wants to. A world class race, the purse for the Governor's Cup is around $15,000. It takes 95 to 100 hours to run it. The entry fee is $175, but it can cost thousands of dollars to get a team ready, considering the cost of the special dog food, gear, traveling, time off from work and the quality of dogs you'll need to run such a race.

Time is perhaps the biggest factor that discourages some people. It takes 1500 miles of training before you are ready to run a 500-mile race, which means many nights of running 100 miles with your dogs instead of watching your favorite TV shows. It also means special diets for the dogs and commitment to the undertaking. You have to train four to five days a week, working up to fifty to 150 miles a day. You start slowly (about five miles per day) and work up to greater mileage as the dogs' strength and endurance increase.

But if you love the sport—go for it! The drivers of the 1,049-mile Alaskan Iditarod train year-round. It costs up to $30,000 to get ready for this race. The purse is $30,000.

FAMILY SPORT

Sled dogs can be fun for the whole family. There is even a "Pee-Wee" class for the youngsters, and they have a ball. It is really a crowd pleaser, watching the kids run their teams, hearing mom or dad yelling at the other and encouraging the dogs to go faster and the kids to "*stop that team!*" at the other end.

The finish chute is always a welcome sight to the driver. It also has a snow fence to keep the teams on the trail and the timer's will stand just at the turn to register the drivers' times crossing the finish line.

This fellow came in without a drivingbow. He also lost a runner. He said it didn't really matter because his team "walked" the last five miles anyway.

This little guy handles two dogs as his parents wait at the other end of the short course. These are our future drivers.

In a related dare-devil sport called ski-joring a driver on a pair of skis is pulled by a team of one, two, or three dogs. I drove my team of three dogs while on skis when I first started in this sport and no one told me you had to STOP them. You *can't* when you are on skis, so someone must be at the other end to stop the team. It is great fun!

There is something for everyone, from camping to racing, to just enjoying your dogs on a cold, crisp day. Use your animals, don't let them sit around and grow old. They love the out of doors and being with you.

Just a sloppy kiss for a friend!

It's nice to have help after a hard day's run.

15
Caring For The Sled Dog

A running dog needs a high protein diet with more fat content than the standard diet. He will burn more calories and needs fat for energy. If you feed a commercial dog food found in the supermarket, add meat and vitamins to it. Make sure the dog is getting what he needs to perform the way you expect. You should feed the best dog food you can afford. It will cost you a little more money, but in the long run it will increase the dogs' performance and give them the needed nutrients. There are a lot of different dog foods on the market today. Reading the ingredients on the package will help you to determine which food is best suited for your working dog. It should have at least 29% protein and 10% fat. The better dog foods have special mixes for working dogs with a high fat level. You can mix ground turkey, chicken, liver, or beef to attain a higher fat level. Chicken and turkey have the highest levels of fat and are easier for the dog to digest. A ground meat additive called "Pet-Pak" has course ground meat and charcoal in it. Ask your pet store owner where to purchase it. The food should be mixed with water—most dogs won't drink enough water in the winter. Sometimes we will bait the water with a can of dog food just enough to encourage the dogs to drink about four cups a day. If you are training hard, they need water so they don't dehydrate.

Drivers are very close to their dogs and spend a lot of time just loving them before a race and making sure they have plenty of water and some shade, if possible, under which to lie down and keep cool. They have to have enough room to lie down. This is Pat Faherty and the dogs he ran in his first race. He and his wife Diana are very close to their dogs and spend a lot of time working with them.

Don't feed or give the dog water immediately after a run; let them cool down first. Try to get them to drink a little *before* the run to keep them from eating snow on the trail.

There are hundreds of stories told on feeding the winning sled dog. Anyone you talk to will have a different way to feed. You must find the food combination that works best for your particular dogs. When we are racing, we usually feed early to let the food digest before the day's run. I feed only once a day. I will feed around five o'clock in the afternoon when I know the dogs will be running early the next morning.

THE FEET OF THE SLED DOG AND THEIR CARE

If you have a long haired dog, clip the hair as short as you can around the lower part of the leg (pasterns), the foot, and between his toes. Ice will stick to this soft hair because a dog perspires through his feet and the warm moisture will cause the ice and snow to stick and form snowballs on the bottom of the feet. This, in turn, causes soreness and can cut the pads of the feet causing lameness. Do the clipping with either a pair of scissors or an electric clipper. I prefer clippers because I can clip the hair closer to the skin.

The breeds that have the most problem with snowballs are Samoyeds, Irish Setters, Airedales, and Standard Poodles. Some of the longer haired Siberian Huskies also have trouble in warm tempratures. I have two "fuzzies,"

98

as we call them, and I have to clip their hair between their toes really short to keep snow from packing. Snow becomes sticky when the temperature rises above 25 degrees. It has the same tendency if temperatures drop to 50 degrees below zero. However, we usually don't have to worry when it gets that cold—we are inside by the fire where we belong and Fido is curled up in his nice warm dog house.

ICE AND SNOW PROBLEMS

If your dogs have problems with cut and sore feet one remedy is to put *Vaseline®* mixed with *Coppertox®* on the foot to keep the snow from sticking. There are other concoctions used, such as *Pam®* oven spray. I use this and it really works for short races and is quite inexpensive.

Scarlet Oil® can be used as an antiseptic wound dressing. Another good ointment is *Protecta-Pad®* , which is good for cracked or bleeding pads.

After applying ointment, put on a bootie to protect the foot while it heals. The most logical preventative measure is to stop your team frequently and check your dogs' feet for ice and snow buildup. However, this isn't always practical—especially during a race.

We have the most problems with ice in the late fall when rain or slushy snow melts and then freezes at night. When the snow melts just enough to make it slush, ice particals form as the temperatures drop and slivers of ice (ice splinters) are broken off as the dogs run. Ice splinters are difficult to detect because you can't really see them, but the dog's pad can become swollen and very sore. Every year new medications for the relief of sore feet appear on the market.

BOOTIES

Booties are made of durable fabric attached to the dog's foot by either *Velcro* or elastic. There are many types of booties on the market, or one can even use a pair of baby socks to protect an injured foot. However, on the trail a much heavier material must be used. I spent all one day making 48 booties out of some denim, only to have them wear out in less than four miles on a gravel road.

Some materials that can be used are *Gore-tex*, polypropylene, canvas, or even a soft leather. They are attached half way up the bootie with a strip of *Velcro* sewn into the side seam. Some drivers tape them on with duct tape.

I have included a simple pattern for making your own booties. This pattern should fit a dog weighing approximately 45 to 60 pounds. Make a sample bootie and try it on your dog then make adjustments to fit.

Booties are used on the trail when the conditions of the trail become icy or when a dog has pulled a toenail or injured his pad while training on dirt. A dog's pad can wear out quickly on a gravel/dirt road, so try to find soft dirt for training trails. Always check your dogs' feet after a run and carry booties with you in case they are needed. Most dogs object to booties at first but soon forget about them when the team is running.

PATTERN FOR BOOTIES

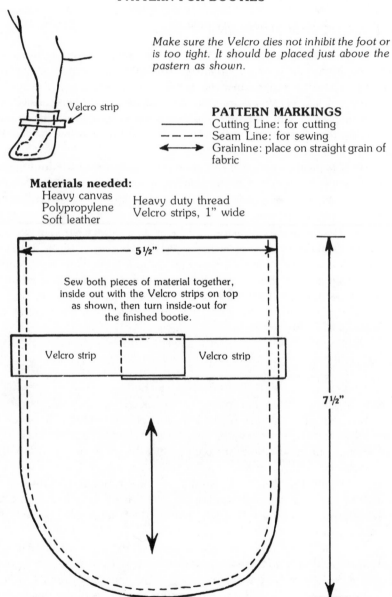

Make sure the Velcro dies not inhibit the foot or is too tight. It should be placed just above the pastern as shown.

Velcro strip

PATTERN MARKINGS
——— Cutting Line: for cutting
- - - - Seam Line: for sewing
← → Grainline: place on straight grain of fabric

Materials needed:

Heavy canvas
Polypropylene
Soft leather

Heavy duty thread
Velcro strips, 1" wide

5 ½"

Sew both pieces of material together, inside out with the Velcro strips on top as shown, then turn inside-out for the finished bootie.

Velcro strip   Velcro strip

7 ½"

NOTE: If a stretch material is being used, place pattern on direction of stretch.

SHELTERS FOR THE OUTDOOR DOG

A shelter can consist of anything a dog can get into to keep out of the wind and weather. However, most of us would agree our dog needs a *real home*, something he can call his own. I have used whiskey barrels, square dog houses, A-frame dog houses and even bought a beautiful commercial dog house, but my dogs still prefer to dig a hole and lie in it. However, when the sun is hot they go into their dog house to keep cool or they will use it if it starts to rain.

Dog houses will vary in size, structure and cost. All a dog needs is someplace where he can curl up to sleep. If the dog house is too small he won't be comfortable; if it is too big it won't keep him very warm.

We make dog houses shaped like little A-frames and fill them with grass-hay. Straw will slip and end up outside, but grass-hay seems to pack better. Hay keep the dogs dry and clean, pulls the moisture from the dog, and keeps the coat clean and fresh smelling.

Whiskey barrels also make good dog houses. Just take one end out and put a little hay inside. This only works if you have small dogs. My larger dogs couldn't get in and turn around. A piece of wood across the bottom of the doorway will keep the hay from being pulled out by the chain.

Don't put carpeting or blankets in your dog's house because they stay damp and can collect disease as well as make your dog smell *doggy*. Never use insulation on the inside of a dog house as the fiberglass could cause serious harm to your dog. Dogs eat things out of boredom so keep plastics and styrofoam away from them.

An empty barrel makes a good shelter.

101

If your dog has a very short coat and chills easily build a larger dog house and put a small light in it. We use a 3-foot x 4-foot house for whelping, and a light in it keeps it really toasty. Make the house deep enough so that the dog can crawl back into it and curl up out of the wind. Face your houses to the south, so the dog will get the most out of the winter sun. (If your major storms come from the south, face the dog's house to the east.) Remember that if the storm comes from the north the snow and wind can whip around a south opening and fill it with snow.

A "Rocky Mountain Chalet."

Appendix

NEWSLETTERS AND MAGAZINES

There are newsletters and booklets that come out each month to let the sled dog enthusiast know what's going on. The *INFO* is put out by the International Sled Dog Racing Association, Inc. and will be sent to you when you join this organization. Write to:

The International Sled Dog Racing Association, Inc.
c/o Donna Hawley
Box 446
Nordman, Idaho 83848-0446

Another mailer is the *TEAM and TRAIL* magazine, it comes out once a month from October to March. Write to:

Publisher/Editor: Cindy Molburg
Center Harbor, New Hampshire 03226

Western Editor: Mel Fishback
Marion, Montana 59925

DIRECTORY OF SLED DOG OUTFITTERS

ADANAC/ZIMA: Jack and Laurie Beckstrom, 4108 Hwy. 93 N., Kalispell, Montana 59901

DOG SLEDS BY MORGAN: Stan Morgan, 17 Mercer Dr., Brampton, Ontario L6X 1B5

FROSTY HILL FARM: Beth Edge, 4480 Hendershot N.E., Grand Rapids, MI 49504.

FRANK HALL SLEDS: Frank and Nettie Hall, 5875 McCrum Rd., Jackson, MI 49201

KEMA SLEDS: Keith Poppert, P.O. Box 415, Wasilla, Alaska 99687

MEL'S CUSTOM HARNESSES: Mel Fishback, 9857 Hwy. 2W, Marion, MT 59925

NEVER SUMMER: Leslie Fields, P.O. Box 8561, Ft. Collins, CO 80524

NORDYKN: Pat Mitchell, P.O. Box 158, Pullman, WA 00163

NOVA EQUIPMENT: Garth Wallbridge, Box 383, Yellowknife, N.W.T. (North West Territory) X1A 2L8

RAE'S HARNESS SHOP: George Rae, 1524 Dowling Rd. #6, Anchorage, AK 99507

ALASKA K-9 SUPPLY: George Rae, 1524 Dowling Rd. #6, Anchorage, AK 99507

TED'S HARNESS SHOP: Ted and Shari Wiktorek, 3631 S. Chase Ave., Milwaukee, WI 53207

TUN-DRA: The Chedles, 16438 96th Ave., Nunica MI 49448

TIM WHITE SLEDS: Rt. T Box 670, Grand Marais, MN 55604

WENEHA: Lynn Chenette, 4518 Malyby Rd., Bothell, WA 98011

These sled dog outfitters will be glad to send you their brochure on the equipment they carry and any information you may need on their equipment. If some of these are no longer in existence, write to another one or contact the ISDRA.

Glossary

ALASKAN HUSKY—Any of the Arctic breeds or northern type dogs with a double coat and curled tails. These dogs can be cross-bred also.

ALASKAN MALAMUTE—The largest of the northern breeds; is also registered with the Kennel Club of America.

BASKET—The cradle in which freight or passengers are carried.

BRIDLE—The line and loop which are attached permanently to the bottom of the sled. The gangline (q.v.) is attached to the bridle.

BRUSHBOW—Curved piece of wood or plastic around the front of the sled to ward off brush and trees.

BUNGIE CORD—Elastic cord placed inside of the gangline or bridle to absorb shocks; or Shock Cord (q.v.)

CHUTE—The starting or finish area of the race.

COLLAR—The leather or nylon strap around the dog's neck.

COME GEE!, COME HAW!—the commands for 180-degree turn, to call a dog back to the driver on the trail.

DOG BOX—A compartment made of plywood that fits onto the back of the truck and holds the dogs securely while traveling.

DOG YARD—The area where breeders keep their kennel and where the dogs are tied.

FOOT PAD—The pad on the runners where the driver stands.

GANGLINE—The line between the dogs. It is attached to the bridle and to each dog by way of the tug and necklines.

GEE—A command for a right turn.

HANDLEBOW—The handle the driver hangs onto on the sled; often called the driving bow.

HARNESS—The nylon gear a dog wears while on a team or pulling a heavy load. Also used for ski-joring.

HAW—The command to turn left.

HIKE—The command to go forward.

HOUND—Any variety of dog not an Arctic breed, regardless of ancestry, unless a specific breed of dog.

INDIAN DOG—Often regarded as a village dog; Alaskan husky of mixed breed from the villages.

LEAD DOG/LEADER—The dog in the front position receiving commands and leading the team.

LINE OUT!—The command to straighten the gangline out and hold it tight.

MUSHER—One who travels over snow with dog team or sled. Also a cart in warmer regions.

NECKLINE—The line between the collar and the gangline.

ON-BY—The command to pass by a turnoff or another sled.

PEDALING—Pushing the sled with one foot while the other remains on the runner.

POINT DOGS—The dogs directly behind the leaders. Also called swing dogs.

QUICK RELEASE—The releasing equipment used to hold a sled or cart in place while hooking up a team. It will release a team quickly.

RIGGING—All the line (gangline) hooked onto a dog and the sled.

RUNNERS—The surfaces on which the sled slides; may be of wood, plastic or steel.

SHOCK CORD—Elastic cord placed inside the gangline or bridle to absorb shocks; or Bungie Cord (q.v.)

SIBERIAN HUSKYS—A medium sized dog (average weight 50 pounds). It is a northern breed and recognized by the Kennel Club of America. Usually has a facial mask.

SLATS—Thin pieces of wood which make up the bottom of the sled's basket.

SNOW HOOK/SNOW ANCHOR—The curved piece of steel in the shape of a hook which is attached to the sled's bridle to hold the dogs.

SNUB LINE—Line attached to the sled, which is used to secure the sled temporarily to a tree or post.

STAKE-OUT CHAIN—The chain used to contain a dog while hooking him up or while he is attached to the truck.

STANCHIONS OR STRUTS—The upright pieces of wood on a sled.

SWING DOGS—The dogs behind the leaders often called the point dogs (q.v.)

TEAM DOGS—Any dogs other than the leaders, point dogs, or wheelers.

TRAIL—Request to pass by a driver who wants right-of-way on the trail.

TUGLINE—The line from the gangline to the dog's harness connecting at the dog's tail.

WHEEL DOGS—The dogs directly in front of the sled or cart.

WHOA—The command to stop.

Want to know more about your dog?

The following titles may be ordered direct, or purchased at your local bookstore or pet supply shop:

YES! Please send me:

Qty.

____**Positively Obedient, Good Manners for the Family Dog.**
Barbara Handler. $8.98

____**How to Raise A Puppy You Can Live With.**
Rutherford & Neil. $7.98

____**Owner's Guide to Better Behavior in Dogs & Cats.**
William Campbell. $10.98

____**Canine Reproduction—A Breeder's Guide.**
Phyllis A. Holst, DVM. $17.98

____**Scent—Training to Track, Search, & Rescue.**
Pearsall & Verbruggen. $15.98

____**Canine Hip Dysplasia and Other Orthopedic Diseases.**
Fred L. Lanting. $14.98

____**What's Bugging Your Dog—A Guide to Canine Parasitology.**
Schneider. $5.98

Please add $2.00 per order under $20.00; $3.00 per order over $20.00. Colorado residents please add 3% sales tax.

☐ Payment enclosed   ☐ Please charge my: ☐ VISA   ☐ Master Card

Acct. #_____ Exp. Date_____

Signature _____

Name _____

Address _____

City_____ State_____ Zip_____

Mail to:

Alpine Publications, Inc., 2456 E. 9th St., Loveland, CO 80537